WOOLLY WORMS & WOMBATS

For The Cullens—
Nothing in this book
measures up to
THE LAKE! Thanks for
being like a second
family to me.

Chris Dann

WOOLLY WORMS
& WOMBATS

A SIDELONG GLANCE AT
FLYFISHING DOWN UNDER

Chris Dawson

Cover and text design: Margaret Donharl

A briefer version of "When the Wind is in the East"
first appeared in *Trout Canada Magazine* under the title
"A Canadian Rises Down Under."

Library of Congress Cataloging-in-Publication Data
Dawson, Chris.
    Woolly worms & wombats: a sidelong glance at flyfishing down
under / Chris Dawson.
        p. cm.
    ISBN 1-55566-121-1
    1. Trout fishing—Australia.   2. Trout fishing—New Zealand.
    3. Fly fishing—Australia.   4. Fly fishing—New Zealand.   I. Title.
    II. Title: Woolly worms and wombats.
SH688.A8D39   1994
799.1'755—dc20   94-3132
                                                                      CIP

1 2 3 4 5 6 7 8 9

Printed in the United States of America by
Johnson Printing Company
1880 South 57th Court
Boulder, Colorado 80301

for Brian,
for Jeanne,
for Chris Clarke,

three pillars of strength
and support

Contents

PREFACE

Flyfishing is under my skin. It's been there for over ten years and there's never been a time in those years that I haven't taken it seriously. It's under your skin, too, or you wouldn't be reading this right now.

In the spring of 1991, I walked into my boss's office at the *Calgary Herald* newspaper. Canada, like the rest of the world, was deep in recession. In an effort to save money, the *Herald* had offered reporters voluntary leaves-of-absence. I asked for ten months.

"I have no problem with the length of time," my boss explained, "as long as you're doing something constructive. I don't want you going to Hawaii to lie on a beach somewhere." I told him I was planning a trip to the Southern Hemisphere. To flyfish. He stared into my eyes for a good long while, and I'm not sure what he saw there. But afterwards, with just the slightest hint of a smile, he said, "Okay, you've got it."

This is not a book about lodges and guides and helicopters. There is some of that, to be sure, but others have thoroughly covered that ground: Ernest Schwiebert and Lefty Kreh, to name two. This is a book about two countries, New Zealand and Australia, and the ordinary, everyday people who live and flyfish for trout in them. The people in these pages opened their homes and their lives to me. They are a bricklayer who rushed home from work every night for a week so that he could share his favorite angling spots with a stranger from around the world, an unemployed Tasmanian who drove me halfway around the island at his expense mumbling "beautiful, beautiful" every time we hooked a fish, and a New Zealand farmer who abandoned the sheep for a weekend so that we could cast flies into a river a hundred miles away. They are people like you and I—people with something under their skin.

That's not to say that flyfishers who stay in lodges and hire guides won't gain anything from these pages, because I think they will. There's something here for everyone. I don't pretend to be an authority on flyfishing. Most assuredly, I'm not. But almost a decade of working in the newspaper business has taught me a thing or two about observation and the subtle—and often *not* so subtle—differences between people and countries.

This is not a flyfishing guidebook in the strict how-to, where-to sense, but where appropriate, I've tried to work as much of that sort of information as possible into the text. The final chapter tackles many of those how-to, where-to questions head on. I should also add a note of caution here: if you're looking for tale after tale of enormous fish landed written with magazine-style hype, then this book probably isn't for you. I've never equated the quality or uniqueness of a fishing experience by the number or size of fish landed, and neither do these pages. To borrow a phrase, this book represents the good, the bad, and the ugly of Down Under trout fishing. Any lengthy angling excursion without at least two of the three would be incomplete. After all, what's a baseball game without a few bobbled balls, a bird hunting trip without a few missed shots? Be assured, there are plenty of bobbled balls in this book—a book about an ordinary, everyday guy whose curiosity dragged him halfway around the world to fish with flies.

Be careful. It could happen to you, too.

PRONUNCIATION KEY

Eucumbene = YOU-kum-bean
Jindabyne = JIN-dah-bine
Kaipo = KIE-po
Kaweka = Ka-WEE-kah
Khancoban = Kan-KO-bin
Kosciusko = KOZ-ee-oz-koh
Makarora = MAH-kuh-ro-rah
manuka = ma-NEW-kah
Maoris = MAUW-reez
Mararoa = MARE-ah-ro-ah
matagouri = mah-tah-GOR-ee
Mohaka = Mo-HAW-kah
Ngaruroro = NAIR-oo-ro-ro
Oamaru = o-AY-ma-roo
Oreti = Or-EE-tee
Rangitikei = Rang-ah-TIC-kee
Rotoiti = Ro-toe-ee-tee
Rotoroa = RO-toe-ro-ah
Rotorua = RO-toe-roo-ah
Taieri = TIE-ree
Taupo = TAUW-po
Tongariro = TAWN-gah-rear-oh
Tumut = TOO-mitt
Urewera = Yer-eh-wair-ah
Waiau = WHY-ow
yobbo = YAH-boh

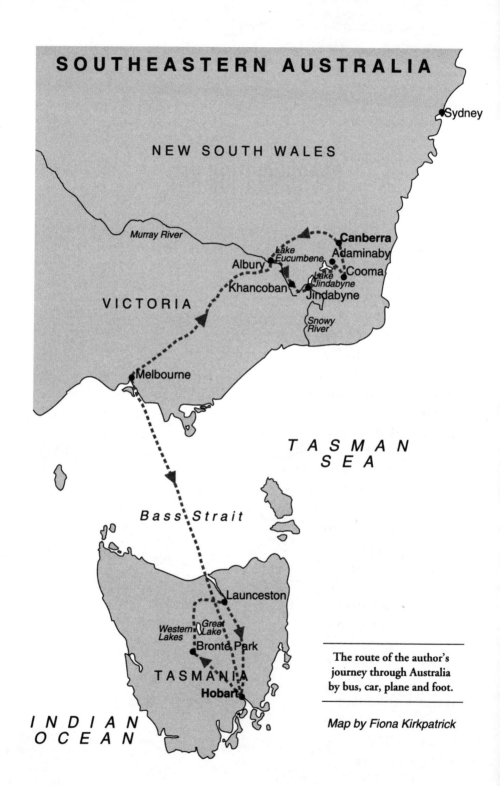

SOUTHEASTERN AUSTRALIA

Sydney

NEW SOUTH WALES

Murray River

Lake Eucumbene

Canberra

Adaminaby

Albury

Cooma

VICTORIA

Khancoban

Lake Jindabyne

Jindabyne

Snowy River

Melbourne

TASMAN SEA

Bass Strait

Launceston

Western Lakes

Great Lake

Bronte Park

TASMANIA

Hobart

INDIAN OCEAN

The route of the author's
journey through Australia
by bus, car, plane and foot.

Map by Fiona Kirkpatrick

PART I - AUSTRALIA

WHERE THERE'S A WILL THERE'S A WAY

I am not sure why, but I always figured kangaroos would be a lot like cows. Not *look* like cows, of course, but generally *act* like cows. I thought they'd do things like hang out in broad daylight and calmly watch people walk by. Maybe lean against barbed-wire fences. That sort of thing.

Well, I was wrong. I discovered that my first day in Australia, traveling on the bus from Melbourne to Albury, and headed straight for, as I was soon to find out, the dean of Australian flyfishing.

"Where are all the kangaroos?" I asked the bus driver. I'd seen a sign outside the window warning motorists about kangaroos crossing the highway. The sign was yellow with the silhouette of a kangaroo on it, much like the deer crossing signs back home.

"You won't see any during the day, mate," he told me. "They're up in the hills. They don't start coming out until dusk. Even then, I reckon the only way to get close to one is with a rifle." Or, apparently, with a car. He went on to explain that kangaroos love to feed along highway ditches after dark. Every now and then one takes a wrong turn and *BANG*—end of kangaroo. It struck me then that one of the major differences between kangaroos and cows is that kangaroos can jump barbed-wire fences and cows can't. If there's a moral here it's that evolution can get you into trouble. I know this firsthand. Some years ago I discovered that humans had evolved to the point where they can cast a fly rod, and in one way or another, I've been in trouble ever since.

That's what I was thinking as the sprawling southeastern Australian foothills rolled by and the Snowy Mountains loomed ever closer. Had I really traveled all this way from Canada to flyfish? Was I an addict? Was I sane? A turtle sunning on a rock slipped into the water and fish were rising in the turbid Murray River next to the twisting, two-lane highway. I decided to direct my questions at the driver instead of myself.

"Are those trout?" I asked him.

"No," he said. "Just cod and trash fish. There are no trout this far down."

The foothills expanded and the river shed weight. Heat distorted the land, land that reminded me of the alternately treed and open pastures back home, and the cloudless, feverish sky appeared smudged as though I were looking through a dirty windowpane. A flock of a dozen or so snow-white birds lit on a power line. They looked like targets in a shooting gallery.

"Are those cockatoos?" I asked the driver.

"Yes," he said. "See the crest on their heads? You'll mostly see white ones, but there are black ones about, too."

We pulled into a small town called Walwa. The local copper, or policeman, was cooling off in a backyard swimming pool with a bunch of kids. "There's obviously not much crime around here, eh, mate?" quipped the driver. "I reckon they don't even lock the bank."

Two tanned sheepskins hung on a clothesline outside a bleached wooden shack. A white-chinned black Labrador wandered out of the shade, satisfied itself that we posed no threat, and retreated. We pulled up to the general store for a soda, but it was closed. "Back at 3," read a sign taped to the door.

As we rounded a corner on the highway, the Snowy Mountains abruptly came into view. It was November in Australia, springtime, and the mountaintops were covered in snow. One of the best things about flyfishing Down Under is that the season is just getting underway as North America braces itself for winter. Anyway, the Aussie heat was paralyzing, and the snow seemed as remote as a postcard held at arm's length. The driver noticed it, too.

"Jesus," he said. "Whadaya say, mate? How 'bout a dose of that!"

"Jesus," I replied.

The next morning I rang the doorbell, and Mike Spry answered dressed in red woollen long johns. They had a convenient little trap door and white buttons down the front. Never mind that it was eight in the morning, that's not important. What *is* important is that I'd managed to track down my sole Australian flyfishing authority. Found him right there in the town of Khancoban where that article in *Flyfishing* magazine said he'd be. I pulled the tattered pages out of my pocket and showed them to him, explaining that I'd come over from Canada and intended to spend a few weeks fishing in the area.

"I was hoping to take a guided float trip," I said.

"*Today?*"

"Well, yeah, but if it's a problem, I can always come back."

"*No!* I mean . . . no, that's okay. Just sit on the porch a second while I put some clothes on. I'll be right out."

I heard rustling inside the house. People getting up. Hushed whispers. I suspected they were discussing my sanity which, under the circumstances, didn't surprise me very much; you'll recall I'd been doing the same thing the day before. Mike reappeared and asked me if I'd like to join them for breakfast. "I'll be damned," he said, as if the thought was just registering. "All the way from Canada."

Let's get one thing straight right now: Mike Spry is to Australian flyfishing what Joe Montana is to American football. Entering his house was like entering the Australian Flyfishing Hall of Fame. There was an entire wall hidden by flyfishing tomes—four hundred at last count. There was an antique rod and reel leaning in the corner. There were loose feathers about, floating in the air. Maybe his business card said it best: W.M. SPRY B. Rur. Sc.—Recreational Freshwater Fishing Consultant.

Okay, so I was intimidated. Who wouldn't be? Mike even *looked* intimidating. Balding and barrel-chested, with a thick silver beard, his eyebrows rose authoritatively when he spoke, reminding me of

Mr. Spock on *Star Trek*. He looked every bit the professor, the only difference being that instead of a ballpoint pen in his shirt pocket, he carried a fly box.

Mike explained that he was busy conducting a one-week flyfishing school, but that his son Will could take me out if I liked. Fine, I said. Guessing him to be in his early twenties, Will was fair-skinned and prematurely balding—something in the genes, I suppose—with the physique of a rugby player and a meaty handshake tenderized by a year away at college. I liked him immediately, and Mike assured me that he knew the Snowy Mountain rivers as well as anyone.

While Mike's wife Margaret made lunch, Will and I loaded a twelve-foot gray inflatable raft with a rowing frame onto the trailer. The next thing I knew we were off, headed for the Swampy Plains River and some of the best brown trout fishing Australia has to offer.

We put in a few miles from town, below the Pondage dam. Because it was at least eighty degrees out, I felt foolish slipping into my heavy nylon chest-waders, but Will said the water was cold and I'd need them. I rolled them down and cinched the shoulder straps around my waist. As we pushed off, Will noted that Mike and a half-dozen budding flyfishers had gathered on the far bank. No doubt to watch the Canadian make a fool of himself, I thought.

"Damn Yankee, go home!" Mike yelled.

"I'm not American," I shouted back. "I'm Canadian."

"All the same," a pupil quipped. The exchange seemed innocent at the time, harmless, in fact, but later in the trip I'd think about it often. Aussies and New Zealanders can be quite blunt in their criticism of Yanks. Canadians, or Canucks, generally fare better, probably because we share the same Queen and all that. The British Commonwealth and royalty have never done much for me except that May 24, a statutory holiday celebrating the anniversary of Queen Victoria's birthday, is usually the time that Kevin Watson and I head off to Montana for the first fishing trip of the year.

As far as the Swampy Plains was concerned, the thing I remember impressing me the most was the clarity of the tailwater below the dam. I don't know why, but it's not the sort of thing I expected in Australia. Too hot, maybe. Too muted. But the water was clear, clear in the sense that juice in a pickle jar is clear—slightly green, slightly brown, mostly none of either. Golden cobblestones lined the riverbed, and wispy strands of green weed wavered in the current.

Will had me tie on a size 14 Royal Wulff. "It's the fly we fish ninety percent of the time," he said. "There's not much of a rise during the day, and the Wulff works as well as anything else." I falsecast a couple of times, then let the fly drift along beside the raft in the middle of the river. We were still within sight of the dam when I hooked the first fish. It was a fourteen-inch brown trout that rose with a choreography usually reserved for fishing videos. Slow and easy. I hopped from the raft to land the fish, and Will reached for my camera.

We were *still* within sight of the dam when I hooked the second fish. Damn, I thought, not bad. It was larger than the first, maybe twenty inches, and it got off at my feet.

"Two fish on and we haven't even gone two hundred meters," Will noted. "I have to warn you though, it's not always like this."

Now, pause for a moment and place yourself in my wading boots. You've just blindly hooked two nice trout in less than fifteen minutes. In Montana, of course, you'd say, "Big deal." But you're not *in* Montana. You're in *Australia*, of all places, a continent that, until you've traveled there and seen it for yourself, a foreigner usually associates with outback deserts, great white sharks, and Crocodile Dundee. Freshwater trout? Hardly. But they're there, and you know that now, because you've held one in your own doubting hands. "I'll be damned," you say to yourself, and you're still within sight of the dam.

The Swampy Plains River briskly winds through broken pasture, weeping willows dangling from the banks and towering red gum eucalyptus branches reaching out to touch the sky. Oz, as Aussies affectionately call their homeland, is famous for its eucalyptus trees. There are over six hundred species there, varying in shape and height as much as the pine and spruce trees do in the U.S. and Canada. The leaves, which are long, narrow, and leathery, contain an oil that supposedly smells like camphor and is used as a deodorant, an antiseptic, and a stimulant.

The only stimulant I needed was the Swampy Plains. The fishing was fast and reactionary, Will barking directions as I spun to one side and then the other to hit the pockets in time. I was trying to take in the scenery and cast simultaneously, but it just wasn't working. I kept thinking of a line by angling writer Paul Schullery: "Calling fishing a hobby is like calling brain surgery a job." Well, I was in the operating room and the patient was dying.

After an hour or two on the Swampy Plains, it started to dawn on me that maybe I'd been there before. But *when?* And then, like a Woolly Bugger smacking into the back of my head, it hit me. The Swampy Plains fished like Montana's Beaverhead River but was more along the size of the Bighorn. Heck, there were even carp in the backwaters.

The dry fly stopped working so I tied on a size 10 San Juan Worm and nymphed from the raft. Will had never seen anything like the Worm. Neither had the fish, which ignored it altogether. "Oh, well," I told Will, "it was worth a try." Suddenly Will pointed to a swirl and shouted, "Platypus!" I turned too slowly, glimpsing brown fur that could have belonged to a muskrat for all I knew. The duck-billed platypus is as uniquely Australian as the koala bear, the Tasmanian devil, and the kangaroo. Every North American kid learns about the platypus in school—a web-footed, primitive mammal that lays eggs. It's one of only two mammals in the world to do so, and the other, the porcupine-like echidna, is also native to Australia. Still, don't go to Oz expecting to see rivers teeming with platypuses and forests full of koalas. I know I expected to. The somber truth is, however, that almost all of Australia's fabled critters are either nocturnal, extremely timid, or on the endangered species list. In almost two months spent fishing there, I never did get a good look at a platypus. I never got *any* look at a wild koala or Tasmanian devil.

I caught a few more fish before lunch, and then we pulled into an eddy behind an overhanging willow. Will took a checkered black-and-white tablecloth and arranged it on the seat in the raft. We spread caviar on crackers and toasted the morning with champagne. The highlight of lunch was a short jaunt through the eucalyptus to an isolated backwater about twenty yards from the river. Two or three nice brown trout swam contentedly in an aquamarine pool. I'd seen bigger hot tubs.

"Try a bow-and-arrow cast," said Will, and I did my best William Tell impersonation. The target was a chunky fifteen-inch brown that casually swam over and took the Royal Wulff. The remaining trout scattered. "Obviously," I told Will, "this is a one-arrow pool."

Later in the afternoon a storm blew in with Bighorn-like ferocity. Will and I ducked into a miniature harbor and crouched while branches blew onto the water and eucalyptus leaves coated the surface. Half an hour later the sun was out again and there wasn't a cloud in the sky.

"Where are all the other fishermen?" I asked. It had suddenly occurred to me that we hadn't seen another boat all day and just two anglers on the bank. Will laughed and said he'd wondered when I was going to mention that. After the initial shock of trout fishing in Australia wore off, he explained, it was a question foreign anglers inevitably brought up.

"This is pretty normal," he said. "It's unusual for us to see another boat." I was flabbergasted. According to the promotional brochures and everything I'd read, the Swampy Plains was *the* blue-ribbon trout fishery in Australia. Any perceived similarity to the Bighorn had just been deep-sixed. Will went on to explain how the river was difficult to access for shore-bound anglers because it runs through private land. The dearth of drift boats, he noted, was just another example of how Australian flyfishing was still in its infancy. In time I'd discover that even in New Zealand you don't see a lot of drift boats on the rivers. By and large, anglers in both countries still prefer to walk and wade, owing in equal parts, I think, to the relatively small size of the best rivers, limited boat access, and, especially in New Zealand, the nature of sight fishing to individual fish.

During another lull I asked Will about the insects. That early in the season, he said, the only consistent rise was in the evening. The daytime grasshopper fishing would pick up later in the summer, Will noted, with favored Aussie patterns including the Snowy Mountain Hopper, O'Briens Hopper, Glen Innes Hopper, and the Muddler Hopper. Any of the North American-style hair hoppers work equally well.

By day's end we'd drifted more than twelve miles to below the confluence of the Swampy Plains and Murray rivers. Just before dark bats began swooping over the black, one-dimensional surface. The charcoal air teemed with what looked to me like white caddisflies but Will described as moths. The bankside foliage compressed and my chest tightened. The experience was surreal; one of those Disneyland rides that rattles the senses and tries the sensibilities.

We left the raft to wade a glassy shallow, and I caught three browns in rapid succession with a tan Elk Hair Caddis. Will reached out and touched my shoulder to frame a picture: it was that dark. About a hundred yards downstream, we heard voices on the bank, and Will expertly guided the raft into shore. Mike and Margaret stood waiting by the van.

The next day Will asked me if I'd like to go fishing with him for a couple of days in the Australian backcountry. "No charge," he added. "This time we go as friends." I jumped at the chance. Will explained that he couldn't get away until the next morning, so I had a free day to explore Khancoban with its six hundred or so residents. The first thing that struck me were the immaculate lawns and flower beds. Australians take great pride in their gardening. The small bungalows lining the quiet streets had meticulously clipped hedges and vines climbing trellises beneath shadow-throwing trees. Even the dogs seemed orderly, more often than not watching me pass with nary a bark. When someone mentioned a couple of days later that Khancoban had won a prize as the comeliest town in the district, I wasn't surprised.

At sunset, after a nap at the inn where I stayed in a hostel, I climbed a hill overlooking the sprawling Khancoban Rose Garden. The fuchsia sky illuminated the delicate red and yellow and white petals as brilliantly as lights on a Christmas tree. The deafening clamor of cicadas, which looked like lime green, oversized grasshoppers, issued from every tree and cranny, and the episode became overwhelming in its sensory excess. It was almost too much; after all, I was new to Australia and my nerves were still raw. I descended the hill and walked back into town.

We were headed for Kosciusko National Park and the upper Tumut River. At least that's what Will said. Completely disoriented, all I knew was that we were hurtling through a stifling eucalyptus forest on a red gravel road about twice as fast as we should have been going. The cicadas were at it again—you could even hear them above the car's engine—and the sky was obscured by a green canopy of branches. Sunlight flickered through the leaves like raindrops falling through a screen.

Will explained that Kosciusko National Park is the ski capital of Australia. I tried to let this sink in. It made about as much sense as the Jamaican bobsled team. At 2,228 meters—they don't measure mountains in feet over there—Mount Kosciusko is the highest peak on the continent. Will said the skiing at resorts like Thredbo, Smiggin Holes, and Perisher Valley can actually be quite good during a heavy snow year, which the past winter had been.

Our bushwalk (that's what Australians call hiking or backpacking) into the Tumut River valley took about an hour and a half. The trees thinned out as we gained elevation, and the path wound through fields of blossoming purple and yellow shrubs and spongy alpine heath. Every so often we'd come across a grove of snow gums, an emaciated eucalyptus with thin, striated trunks and scaly bark. Basically, it's the Aussie plant kingdom's version of a shedding zebra. The bottom of the Tumut River valley was exposed and treeless. Over the millennia the river has carved a deep groove for itself, and the valley was uneven with jagged outcrops, peat mounds, and grass tussocks.

Will and I pitched a tent where a small spring-fed stream tumbled down from the brush and into the Tumut. The water was clear and cold, and a welcome sight to two thirsty bushwalkers. The Tumut was clearer than the Swampy Plains; the slight brownish tinge was probably due to the light reflecting off the rust-colored cobblestones of its bottom more than anything else. Above our campsite the river was smooth and straight, about thirty feet wide, and inviting. Below us it constricted into a steep-walled canyon that seemed far less accessible. We instinctively knew that the bigger fish would be in the gorge, but we decided to tackle that reach the next day.

We headed upstream and the fishing was tough. There were no bugs on the surface and nothing was showing. Will said that like the alpine rivers in New Zealand, there really isn't much point in nymphing blindly in Australian headwaters because the fish population doesn't warrant it. Each pool and run holds a couple of wild trout and that's it. Later on in my trip, I'd find those alpine rivers in New Zealand, with their characteristically light or gray-colored bottoms, provided easier sight fishing than the Tumut with its hazel riverbed.

Will and I each tied on a Royal Wulff and went prospecting over likely looking water. Twenty minutes later Will took a beautiful twenty-one-inch brown from a shallow riffle. The fish had thick dark spots over the length of its body and the large, humped back of a healthy wild trout. He hooked and lost another big brown about an hour later. As for myself, I'd made far too many casts before finally enticing a fish at the head of a swirling eddy. I was so surprised when it struck that I didn't give it time to take the hook and yanked the fly out of its mouth. Will was watching from the bank by that time and expressed his condolences. There wasn't much else to say.

After supper we lay on our backs around a small fire. He tried to convince me that fishing amongst deadly snakes was preferable to fishing amongst grizzly bears, and I tried to convince him of the opposite.

"Tell me about *wolves?*" he asked.

"Tell me about dingoes?" I replied.

"*Cougars?*"

"Wombats?"

"*Arctic grayling?*"

"Barramundi?"

We compared notes in our classroom under the stars, two people from opposite sides of the world with a lot of questions and not enough time to answer them all. Life seems short at a time like that and you want to complain to someone that you're being ripped-off. But the sky is clear and the air is cool in your lungs and the grass tickles your neck, and the realization hits home that maybe you haven't been shortchanged after all. Maybe you should be grateful. "Thank you," you mutter, and you're not sure if you're talking to yourself or to Will or maybe to someone else. "Thank you."

The night was cold; by morning the water in the pots had frosted over. After breakfast we hiked well downstream of the gorge to work our way back along the river. The Tumut was deeper there and the pools more pronounced. They were turquoise green, and unlike the day before, we immediately spotted fish. Catching them, of course, was another matter. Without cover along the banks, we stood out pitiably. Accustomed to looking up for danger in the narrow gorge, the fish spotted us before we could spot them. Eventually we just gave up in the midday sun and headed downstream to where the river leveled out.

Finally, in an eddy line around a small bend, we came across three or four rising fish. Will bent over and inspected the water. "Flying ants," he mumbled. I didn't have any flying ants in my fly box, but he did. We took turns wading and casting flying ants at the trout for the next thirty minutes. I'd sit on the bank and then he'd sit on the bank, and each time our turn came up we'd creep forward a little in that way that rejected flyfishers do, hoping that the other fellow hadn't noticed. Which, of course, he had.

"If you get any closer you're going to be standing on them," Will remarked. A sarcastic rejoinder welled up in my throat, but I knew he was right. We made a hasty pact, backed up five paces, and changed flies. Naturally, I hooked a scrappy brown on the *very next* cast. I used a tan Elk Hair Caddis and there wasn't a sedge within miles. At least not one that wasn't peacefully relaxing in a shrub somewhere.

You probably know the next part. Will tied on a tan Elk Hair Caddis and *didn't* hook a fish. In fact, he tried gray, olive, black, and white Elk Hair Caddis and didn't hook a fish with any of those, either. By now the trout were getting edgy, and eventually we put them all down. You'd probably get moody too if someone spent an hour throwing a lasso at your head. I guess you could call it an unproductive afternoon in terms of fish, but the sideshows more than compensated for the disappointing main attraction. I was casting to the tail of a pool when something poked its head over the sloping bank. I wheeled and was face to face with an oversized, gold-colored coyote.

"Will!" I shouted, but the misfit had bolted by the time I could get the word out. I scrambled up the bank as fast as I could in rolled-down waders to see if I could spot it again. "Quick! Come take a look at this." Its pale butt was disappearing down the valley.

He never did see it. From my description, he said it must have been a dingo. Australia's native dog, the dingo arrived with the Aborigines forty thousand years ago and may be an original ancestor of domestic dogs. Ironically, its habit of preying on domestic farm animals has proved to be its downfall. Many farmers will shoot one outright given the chance. Sound familiar?

The next animal to emerge on the Australian bestiary roll-call was a wombat. This one was dead. It lay on the ground in a furry black heap. Blow flies buzzed around its head, and although it seemed intact, death had felled it in the middle of the path. Alive, the nocturnal wombat looks a little like a black bear cub without the pointed snout and ranges in color from silver to brown. Its claim to fame is twofold: first, as a burrowing marsupial (young are carried in a pouch), wombats leave Frisbee-sized holes scattered around the countryside. The fear isn't that a horse will break a leg in one of these things; it's that it will break its *neck*. Second, because wombats have short, stumpy legs and a low center of gravity, they can do serious damage to a car's wheel alignment. Predictably, their lives are not highly regarded.

Neither are the lives of kangaroos. I had finally gotten to see a herd—what do you call a bunch of kangaroos, anyway?—of them on the drive out with Will. It was sunset, just like that bus driver had said it would be, and Will pulled the car over so I could give them a thorough once-over. They milled about a couple of hundred yards away. A little one, called a joey, hopped over to its mother and leapt into her pouch as easily as you'd slip change into a pocket. The mature females were reddish brown and about five feet tall. About three million kangaroos are legally culled each year in Australia, and just as many are killed for sport or by farmers dissatisfied with the government's quota. The truth is they're considered a pest.

I said my goodbyes to the Sprys and hitched farther east to the Snowy Mountain resort of Thredbo, a summer bushwalking hub and winter playground for Australia's rich and famous. Hitchhiking in Oz is generally quite easy, especially in the more remote areas of the countryside and mountains. But more on that in the last chapter. The white van that picked me up was full of rafters headed for the whitewater on the Geehi River. Along the way we startled an emu and its chicks out of the ditch. Second in size only to the African ostrich, emus are shaggy-feathered, flightless birds noted for their curiosity. It struck me as strange to see a five-foot bird running through a mountain forest bereft of conifers, but then, in Australia you quickly get used to things like that.

You'll recall there's a ski area at Thredbo; it was quite impressive by anyone's standards. Twenty feet of snow lingered in the crevices and bowls at the mountaintop, and die-hard skiers and snowboarders still shouldered their gear to give the snow fields a final go. This seemed strange because the valley along the Crackenback River was in full bloom, and golfers had begun hacking away at the grass on the eighteen-hole course. It was a time of transition.

The resort itself was like a small Aspen or Banff—timbered, touristy, and tasteless. The motels and lodges were tiered along the steep hillside. So was the international youth hostel, where I stayed. German and Swiss and British travelers were there; many spent the afternoons lounging on the sun deck that faced the other side of the valley and the ski hill. The evenings were my time to be keen. Grabbing my fly rod, I'd wander down to the river to fish for the small hatchery-raised rainbow trout while the last of the golfers swung away in the purple twilight. The winter had left the fish hungry and unselective, and they rose freely to any small, well-presented dry fly. After dark I'd wander back up to the hostel.

"Well," the travelers would ask me, "where are all the fish?"

"I put them all back," I'd say, knowing they didn't believe me. And who can blame them? Catch-and-release hadn't exactly caught on in Oz, a country, I was finding out, where angling success was gauged by sharp knives and frying pans.

On the third night the fishing came to an end. I broke my rod. I'd like to say that I rolled down a cliff or stumbled in the stream, but that's not the way it happened. I was taking the four-piece rod down in the hostel and struggling to get two sections apart. The tip swung against a concrete wall and snapped. Fighting back tears and hating myself for being so stupid, I held a section of splintered graphite in my hand. It was third generation and, as far as my rod was concerned, the lineage had come to an end.

After a couple of weeks here, I'm slowly starting to adapt to the Aussie way of life. Well, maybe not so much the way of life as the pace of life.

I've begun to think of it in terms of a video recorder. Back in North America, you get up in the morning, hit "play" and, hopefully, away you go. But things are different here. Instead of "play," everyday life cruises along at "slow" or, if there's a pub or another distraction nearby, such as a trout stream, maybe even "pause."

Australia is a country where people still drive the speed limit on highways—where time passes not by the hour hand on a clock but by the passage of the sun across the sky and, if you're a flyfisher, by the metronomic rhythm of a fly rod.

There's beer here, lots of it. Aussies rank right up there with the Germans, Belgians, and Czechs as the biggest consumers in the world. Each state has its favorite brand, from XXXX (or "four-ex," but also called barbed-wire, for obvious reasons) in Queensland to Vic Bitter (or VB) in Victoria. Things can get confusing because the states often call the same brand by different names. Things can also get dangerous, because the rivalry between Aussie states is no different than, say, the rivalry between two college football teams.

Order the wrong beer in a small town in the middle of nowhere, and you're liable to find yourself headed out the swinging door with a leather boot firmly planted on your rear end.

With all that beer around, it isn't surprising that Aussies have come up with about two dozen ways to drink it. You can always drink straight from the bottle, or stubby, but if you want draft beer in a receptacle you're going to have to choose between a glass, goblet, pony, middy, schooner, or pot, depending on how thirsty you are and where you're traveling.

In Victoria you can also order a "5" or a "7," depending on the ounces in the glass. When you think about it, it's not much different than going into a flyfishing shop and being confronted with a rack of rods ranging from a one-weight all the way up to a thirteen-weight. The same way a two-weight might be perfect for those calm evenings on a small stream, a "5" is just the ticket for a quick stopover at the bus depot between rides. And while a thirteen-weight will go the distance with just about anything that swims, spend an evening pounding back schooners with a typical Aussie and you won't be going anywhere.

A SHRIMP ON THE BARBIE

The trendy sportswear shop was a bit expensive for my tastes, but the owner was a budding flyfisher and we got to talking and—well, you know how it is. The owner, Murray, had spotted me across the store carrying the new $50 glass rod (about $70 Aussie dollars) I'd just picked up down the block. It was a far cry from the Sage I'd broken a couple of days earlier, but still better than nothing.

Anyway, we "earbashed" for about an hour before the lone clerk was on the verge of mutiny, and the neglected customers were getting downright edgy. When he finally noticed what was going on, Murray did what any honorable shop owner would do; grabbing me by the arm, he made a beeline for the front door.

"Come on out to my car," he told me. "I have something for you." We strode into the parking lot, and Murray, reaching across the front seat, handed me a tear-and-water-resistant fishing map of the local lakes and rivers.

"I just picked it up this morning, mate," he explained. "But you'll be needing it today, and I can get another one after work. Take it. It's yours." I fished around in my pocket for change, but Murray wouldn't accept anything for the map. Before leaving, he asked where I was staying in town. I told him I'd pitched a small yellow and blue tent at the local caravan, the Aussie equivalent of a trailer park.

"Well," he said, "maybe I'll run by some evening, and we can try our luck at the lake."

It was the sort of comment you hear all the time on a trip like mine—well intentioned but token—and, despite the gift, I really didn't expect to see Murray again. I spent most of the day doing the errands that I'd been putting off and acquainting myself with Jind-abyne, a dry, dusty, hilly Australian town of about fifteen hundred people on the eastern edge of the Snowies. Traveling there from Khan-coban, which was on the other side of the mountains and was, you'll recall, quite verdant, was a bit like driving from Ennis, Montana, over to Fort Smith on the Bighorn River. They may only be a few hundred miles apart, but geography-wise, they might as well be on opposite sides of the world.

Many Aussies regard Lake Jindabyne as the finest stillwater rain-bow and brown trout fishery on the mainland. For scores of Victori-ans, Canberrians, and New South Welshmen, the sprawling reservoir is a trout angler's oasis in an otherwise parched and peeling landscape. A mainstay. Predictable, reliable, and, in Oz, as close as I was going to get to a *sure thing*. The caravan was right on the lake shore, and I planned to use it as a jumping-off point for several fishing trips over the next couple of weeks.

Walking back to the tent with an armload of groceries that eve-ning, a small car startled me by roaring up from behind and slamming on the brakes. Out jumped Murray, telling me to hop in for a lift to the caravan. He said that Wayne, a good friend of his and an avid fly-fisher, had asked Murray if I'd be interested in going over to his place for a few stubbies and a late barbie, or Down Under barbecue.

Thankfully, Murray had spotted me walking along the road after finding my tent vacated at the caravan. We dropped the groceries off, gathered up some gear, and headed up the hill to Wayne's two-story flat. Inside, up a steep flight of stairs, red brick walls supported a high, sloping ceiling with rough timber beams. Outside, a small propane barbecue sent plumes of greasy blue smoke drifting off the balcony, which overlooked the lake. The view was spectacular, sullied only by a grotesque power pole and its bulbous transformer.

Across the nearest bay, Wayne pointed out a rocky, sparsely treed hillside where feral goats often gathered in the evenings to languish in the last shafts of orange sunlight. No matter where I ventured in Australia, the idea of domesticated animals gone wild continued to fascinate me; maybe it was a throwback to devouring Jack London and *The Call of the Wild* when I was a kid. Goats, horses, dogs, cats, pigs, birds, and rabbits—Australia is inundated with feral creatures. Sadly, both there and in New Zealand, the non-native animals do a great deal of damage to native species and to the vegetation. A farm cat striking out on its own during a harsh Canadian winter, of course, wouldn't make it past the barn. But because of the moderate Australian climate and the dearth of natural predators, Kitty stands a pretty good chance of surviving should he decide to pick up and leave the Down Under homestead. Still, that doesn't seem to have stopped Aussies and Kiwis (New Zealanders) from enjoying their pets, because there are plenty around.

During supper, Wayne told me he was a mason who worked seasonally and fished continually. That explained the brick walls; it also explained why he had three fly tying vises and enough materials to stock a small flyfishing shop. Actually, Wayne began fly tying as a hobby before he'd ever cast a line, and his flies stack up against the best I've seen anywhere. You could see his eyes glazing over and his rod hand twitching as we swapped fishing stories with the unceasing flow of a chattering stream. Then suddenly, without warning, Wayne leapt to his feet and proposed a fishing trip.

"*Now?*" Murray replied, dumbfounded. His stubby was still half full.

"Sure," Wayne said. "Why not? The three of us can jump in my ute and go night fishing up at Waste Point." A ute is an Aussie "utility vehicle," generally a pickup car or truck. I was keen, of course, but Murray had his work and marriage to worry about, in that order. He thought it over for a full five seconds, then ran down to get his gear from the car.

It dawned on me that night that Wayne and Murray were angling's odd couple. Murray had a beard and thick glasses and, owing to the sportswear shop, dressed like a Patagonia salesman, always decked out in the latest fleece and cotton. Despite his momentary lapse that evening, his marriage appeared to be sound.

Wayne, on the other hand, had hawk-like, chiseled features, resembled that guy who models Simms waders in all the fishing catalogs, and judging from the response he got whenever we walked into a pub together, had half the sheilas in town contemplating his every move. He was single and loved every minute of it.

Later that evening I was standing knee-deep in the dark waters of Lake Jindabyne, casting blindly with an old seven-weight Wayne had plucked from a stack of rods in the corner. It saved me having to initiate my new $50 special. Wayne's rod had a slow action and the invisible Woolly Bugger whistled dangerously past my ear as I tried to work the kinks out of the loop and my resolve. The wind that had been blowing all day had vanished. The trout, reassured by the onset of darkness, began gliding into the shallows to gorge on the midnight buffet.

I could hear them slurping on something or other, but be damned if I could figure out what they were taking. Lake Jindabyne may have had its share of trout, I thought, but calling it a sure thing was like planning a wedding before the first date. Wayne and Murray must have been having similar problems, because every once in a while a thin beam of light from a headlamp or a flashlight appeared on the shoreline, illuminating a frustrated expression.

Out on the bay a duck squawked and flapped its wings. The sky was clear, but across the lake, heat lightning danced on the horizon like a flickering campfire. I tilted my head back and stared at the celestial light show. The Southern Cross hung in the sky like a bent crucifix. One constellation in particular caught my eye. In the Northern Hemisphere we'd call it Orion, the hunter, but in the Southern Hemisphere it's inverted and known as the Saucepan. To a native North American it was a little unnerving to think of the belt and dagger as a pot and handle, but then who are we to think that we can decide which way is up and which way is down, anyway?

I was beginning to get carried away with thoughts of global significance and personal perspective when it dawned on me that, any way I chose to look at it, I was still just a confused flyfisher standing in a huge puddle with rubber boots on. Reeling in, I trudged down the bank to meet Wayne and Murray.

On the way back to Jindabyne, studiously keeping an eye out for wayward kangaroos along the highway, Wayne asked if I'd like to stay at his place for a few days while fishing in the area. "You can sleep on the couch," he said. "And I'll give you a key so you can come and go as you like." I jumped at the chance (who wouldn't?), and we stopped at the caravan so I could throw my tent and gear into the ute. Back at his flat he gave me a stack of American flyfishing magazines to read, grabbed a quick snack, and said good night. Crawling into my sleeping bag on the couch, my mind turned philosophical again, pondering the kindness of strangers.

I wonder if I'd do the same thing for someone back home, I asked myself, and the answer wasn't as clear cut as I would have liked. I like to think of myself as a trusting person, but the distorted North American ethic and having worked as a reporter ("journo" in Oz lingo) for ten years have left me somewhat jaundiced. I'd have to think long and hard before laying out the welcome mat for a relative stranger, even if he were a flyfisher.

A cycle had been set in motion. Each evening, Wayne rushed home from work—sometimes alone, sometimes with a buddy—so that we could set off and fish until dark. I never would have believed that an area so dry could hold such an array of angling potential. Within a forty-five-minute drive in any direction, we had our choice of lakes, rivers, and streams. One night we'd be casting to stillwater rainbows along a flooded lake shore, the next creeping through the willows along a brook no wider than a hockey stick is long. If there was one constant, it was the weather. Each sunset was as clear and calm as the last, each outing memorable in its own right but made more so by being one of a string of excursions linked with the intricacy of a finely woven net.

I've never fished along an English chalk stream, but if I get the chance some day, I don't imagine it will be much different than the Moonbah River in New South Wales. The Moonbah is the sort of river flyfishers travel to in order to test their mettle. Just when you think you're getting the hang of flyfishing, catching most of the fish cast to and turning your head to stare in awe at your tight loops, along comes a Moonbah. Although it meanders through relatively exposed farmland, its banks are dense with willows. Tall reeds extending out into the water wreak havoc with line control and make roll casting impossible. And granted, while there *are* meadow stretches along the river that an angler can retreat to if necessary, the largest brown trout predictably sip flies along the most difficult-to-access sections.

Wayne handed me an eight-foot, four-weight Loomis IM6 the first time we tackled the Moonbah; I felt like a conductor waving a baton in the air with the whippy rod in my hand. Murray had a five-weight, and Wayne, ever the host, peered over our shoulders and whispered directions. It was impossible to see the fish in the murky water, but as soon as the sun touched the horizon, the trout turned on as if someone had flipped a switch.

Murray, his purple fleece pullover glowing in the saffron light, took up a spot several yards from me along the same bank. The cows grazing on the other side of the river took our presence for granted, as if three anglers were part of the everyday scenery. *My* sights were set upon one trout in particular. Tucked against the far bank, it rose steadily as I tried to make the thirty-foot cast without hanging up on a piece of grass, flower, or shrub on my backcast. After cursing a dozen inanimate objects and inadvertently standing on the line a few times, I finally managed to drop a size 18 *Baetis* imitation in the vicinity of the fish. The cast was far from perfect, landing a few feet outside the trout's feeding lane, but the brown must have been on the lookout because it sent a swirl of water drifting downstream as it swung sideways and gulped the fly.

Even with the four-weight, I managed to keep the fish away from snags before realizing that I had no way to land it. The cattail-like reeds extended at least four or five feet out into the deep water, making it impossible to work the brown to the bank. And since I wasn't about to plunge into the stream a la Paul Maclean in *A River Runs Through It,* the fish and I reached a stalemate; it lying unseen in the security of the reeds; myself standing on the bank holding a stationary fly rod. Rather than just stand there and amuse the cows any longer, I yanked upwards with the rod until the leader came free *sans* fish. End of episode.

Murray, on the other hand, was having better luck. I watched him climb into the heart of a willow tree and dangle a fly over a feeding trout with the dexterity of a monkey peeling a banana. The fish took, Murray hollered, and the fight was on. He landed the trout, a mere runt of eight inches or so, by hauling it from the river, its body cartwheeling as he nabbed it with an outstretched hand. Murray removed the hook from its tiny mouth and slipped the brown back into the water like a slab of butter. The smile on his face was larger than the fish.

The three of us worked our way upstream and came to a forested section of the river where, ironically, the banks opened up, grassy and dark under a canopy of eucalyptus branches high above. I landed and lost about half a dozen browns in less than an hour, including a couple over fourteen inches, and thereafter, when earbashing with Wayne and Murray, referred to the Moonbah as a "great" river and not just a "frustrating" one.

The last fishing trip I made with Wayne was to a small unnamed creek somewhere near the Moonbah. (At least he told me it was unnamed. Of course, I'll never know.) He proposed the trip on a scorching Sunday afternoon. Rather than sweat to death over sluggish fish, Wayne sat down at a vise and set about tying several Goddard Caddis while we waited for the sun to lose momentum. Come evening, he placed the familiar four-weight in my hand and off we went. The unnamed stream wound through a valley covered in sage-like scrub, and Wayne cautioned me to watch carefully where I stepped because of the poisonous copperhead snakes' fondness for the area. (The Australian copperhead is unrelated to the North American snake of the same name.) The stream, no wider than a small irrigation ditch, held both rainbows and browns—the former able to survive because the stream's origin is a cool spring. Ah, yes . . . spring creek fishing in the Australian foothills. Once again, who would have guessed?

Walking behind Wayne I couldn't take my eyes off the giant insect embroidered on the back of his fishing vest. It was a Fuzzy Wuzzy (a bit like a Woolly Worm, another popular Aussie wet fly) done by a girlfriend. The red-and-black pattern had held up quite well over time; not so the girlfriend, who hadn't been heard from in years.

Here's a guy, I was thinking, whose ex-girlfriend takes hours sewing a fly on the back of a dirty flyfishing vest. Either he's incredibly persuasive or the best lover in the state.

The stream was narrow enough to step over in places, but because of the deep water, it was a step that you wouldn't want to miscalculate. Wayne went on ahead, leaving me three or four nice pools and long, placid stretches with undercut banks. The surface was so smooth that I had to toss a blade of grass into the stream to convince myself that it was flowing in the direction Wayne had said it was. I tied on one of Wayne's caddis flies, not because there were any bugs about, but because tossing a nymph or wet fly into the stream would have been like throwing a rock through a pane of glass.

The first two pools yielded nothing. Working upstream, I walked through the knee-high grass along the bank and cast over a narrow run. The stream was no more than five feet wide there and overgrown on either side. Dropping the fly onto the water was like sinking a twelve-foot jump shot with a man in your face. I'd cast, let the fly sit for a few seconds . . . twitch, let it sit for a few more seconds . . . then pick up, move up a few steps, and try again. On about the third or fourth repetition a six-inch rainbow appeared from nowhere and took the fly. The struggle lasted all of ten seconds, the submissive trout lying in the water at my feet after skipping across the surface like a stone. I pulled the bushy fly from its jaw and the runt vanished in a silver flash.

Although Wayne assured me he'd caught a few lunkers in the stream, the fish we caught that day were all about the same size—eight inches or so—and the sensation wasn't unlike plucking feathers from a bird. Still, there's a lot to be said for small-stream fishing. The fish are smaller, to be sure, but so is everything else: the rods, the flies . . . the expectations. And because it takes just as much skill to beguile a ten-inch brown trout in close quarters as it does to double-haul a Jock Scott to a waiting salmon, the small-stream flyfisher deserves equal billing among the sport's fraternity.

I caught a few more small trout then rejoined Wayne farther up the creek. We sat on a couple of boulders overlooking a large pool, waiting for an evening rise that didn't materialize. The eastern sky was beginning to turn deep purple; the western sky faltered like a dying candle. A chill sent a quiver through my torso.

"Wayne," I began, "thanks for all you've done for me. You and Murray, I . . . "

"Mate," he cut me off, "you'd have done the same. When I come to Canada, you can do the same for me."

We sat in silence again and I thought of the night at Lake Jindabyne—of Orion, the hunter, and of the Saucepan. Upside down. Rightside up.

Since English is the official Australian language, you take it for granted that you'll understand what people are saying there. But that's not always the case. For starters, Aussies speak with a nasal drawl and pepper their language with diminutives: blow flies are blowies; a can of beer is a tinny; a university is the uni. Listened to singly, the words' meanings can usually be deciphered. But string a few of them together, get an Aussie to start earbashing, and good luck!

In addition to Oz-speak, which supposedly gets worse the farther one travels into the outback, or "back o' Bourke," another thing to watch out for is the strange Aussie idiom. The familiar yield traffic sign reads Give Way in Oz. I was driving down a highway once when I came across the following sign: Do Not Sleep While Driving. Since the shoulders along the highway were almost nonexistent, I assumed it meant not to pull over for a nap. Later I learned that long driving distances through monotonous terrain led to many drivers falling asleep at the wheel.

However, several months afterwards I read a Canadian newspaper article that suggested another explanation. It mentioned a man from the province of Ontario who was acquitted of murder because he was sleep-walking while committing the offense. The twist is that the man allegedly drove over ten miles to his in-laws' home, stabbed and bludgeoned his mother-in-law to death, and injured his father-in-law—all while sleeping. Like the sign says, Do Not Sleep While Driving.

In time, I came to understand most of what Wayne, Murray, and company were saying. But just when I thought I had this lingo thing all figured out, Wayne had another barbie and invited Greg, a local bartender whose accent was a "no hoper." The party was winding down, the booze was running low, I was trying hard not to "chunder" my supper into the "loo," and then Greg saw me heading for the kitchen.

"Hey, mate, grab me a cake out of the fridge, will ya?" he asked, the words practically dripping from his nose. I said no problem and rummaged in the fridge for something resembling dessert. There wasn't a thing.

"Hey, Greg," I shouted, *"there's no cake in here. Come and see for yourself."*

"Fair go!" he shot back, shaking his head in disgust. "The door, mate. It's in the bloody door!" But it wasn't in the door, at least as far as I could tell. Tired of waiting, Greg pushed his chair back and strode over to the fridge.

"Here," he said, reaching in and grabbing a bottle of Coke. "Cake!" I burst out laughing, explaining to him that I'd been searching for a slice of angel food or Black Forest. That got a good chuckle out of the partygoers. As for myself, I felt like an absolute "dill."

GOLDFISH ON THE FLY

The Australian trout is a hapless victim of domestic abuse. At best, it's ignored and left to fend on its own. At worst, it's maligned and thrashed indignantly.

Nowhere is this abuse more evident than at Lake Jindabyne. Jindabyne's trout are a testament to perseverance. How they've been able to cope in a lake with features like Waste Point, Stinky Bay, Mill Creek Inlet, and Copper Tom Reach is anyone's guess. Of the half-dozen rivers draining into the lake, including the Snowy, only one, the Crackenback, remains unchecked by dams or other obstructions. Jindabyne's plight is so severe that the Monaro Acclimatisation Society, which manages the local fisheries, has begun concentrating its battle for water quality at nearby Lake Eucumbene, having given up Jindabyne as already too polluted and developed to salvage. And yet, somehow, Jindabyne's trout keep coping—keep rising above the muck.

I didn't need to spend too many hours along Jindabyne's shores before sensing that something was wrong. Stinky Bay stank. And near the town, within walking distance of Wayne's place, a number of storm sewers dumped effluent into the bay. The shoreline was littered, the water near town often discolored a sickly blue-green—the same color you get after dumping a cup of toilet cleaner into the bowl. At the other end of the lake, at Waste Point, a flyfisher's most interesting catch of the day was liable to be snagged during the backcast. Great trash heaps lined the grassy bank, industrial garbage spilling over and running into the lake like water. Oil drums lay rusting in the shallows.

"This lake's in real trouble," Wayne conceded during one of our fishing excursions. "I've even seen raw sewage seep into the lake from septic tanks along the shore."

He also pointed out that over the last couple of years, Jindabyne's trout had been threatened by a mid-summer algal bloom that was starving the lake of oxygen. Making matters worse, careless anglers using common goldfish as bait had either accidentally or purposefully introduced the aquarium dwellers into the lake, and the population had exploded. Brown and rainbow trout ripped into the goldfish in the shallows, and if not for the enduring embarrassment, I might have been tempted to tie a handful of bright orange Zonkers and give it a try. Sure, the goldfish were funny then, but as Wayne noted, nature's scales had been tipped and people probably wouldn't be laughing by the turn of the century. Besides, what was next? Piranhas?

As dismal as things seemed, however, Lake Jindabyne is actually just a small part of a rotten whole. In short, the Australian fishing ethic needs a vital shake-up. Aussies want their fish and they want to be able to eat them, too. Catch-and-release is as foreign to them as the Tasmanian Devil is to us; bag limits as high as ten or twelve trout per person per day are the rule rather than the exception; the use of bait is limited only by the imagination and what an angler's spouse will allow in the refrigerator.

Lake Eucumbene, located about twenty miles north of Jindabyne, is shaped like a giant amoeba with its numerous arms, reaches, coves, and inlets. I was standing in a shallow bay there one afternoon, double-hauling a large streamer to cover as much water as possible, when four anglers pulled up on the beach in two cars and cracked open their beers. Country music blared from a pair of speakers perched atop a roof. Each angler had rigged two spinning rods and propped them up in front of the cars with stumps and rocks. It was illegal to fish with more than one rod per angler at Lake Eucumbene, but since the local enforcement officer's marked boat was tied up outside the campground pub a few hundred yards away, the four anglers didn't seem too concerned.

I was falling into the trance-like state indicative of an incredibly slow day when I hooked a small rainbow. The front-seat anglers noticed the bend in the rod and hopped out to investigate.

"Good on ya, mate!" one shouted from shore. I didn't have a net so I backed the fish into the shallows to release it. "I've got a big stick if you reckon you'll need it," said another angler. I told him that I planned to release the fish.

"What?" he mumbled. "Why would you want to do a bloody thing like that?"

The bloody thing, I explained, would be to kill the fish. I repeated that I planned to release it. The four anglers shuffled their feet a bit and held a hushed conference.

"Well, mate," one said, "why not give it to us then?" But no sooner were the words out than I'd slipped the hook from its jaw and steadied the trout before it darted away. The four anglers stared at me as if I'd just committed a crime, which, in their eyes, I'm sure I had. During the ensuing silence I glanced over at the officer's boat and quickly calculated my chances of making it to the pub before being run down by a car trailing a pair of speakers along the beach.

"You fuckin' yobbo," one of them sneered. I was ready for trouble, but the hostile quartet paid me a few more compliments, then ambled back to their cars. I decided I'd had enough fishing for the afternoon and, given the circumstances, made a beeline for the pub.

"What's a yobbo?" I asked the bartender, who politely explained that, depending on the context, a yobbo is roughly equivalent to an asshole. Hell, I thought to myself, I've been called worse by my mother.

It would be nice if we yobbos in North America could package Trout Unlimited and send it priority post to Australia. During the time I spent fishing with Will Spry in the Snowies, he admitted to me once that he had no idea how many trout per mile there were in the Swampy Plains River, which, you'll recall, may be the best brown trout stream on the mainland. The problem, he said, was that no one had ever bothered electroshocking to find out. Everybody just assumed the river was full of trout, and why meddle with a good thing? Never mind that the limit was ten trout per day, bait was welcome, and licenses were free.

Licenses were free, Will went on to explain, because word had it that the state politicians were pressured into dropping fees a few years back by their misguided cronies. Can you imagine free fishing in Montana? The governor wouldn't be able to saddle his horse fast enough to escape the flying fly rods.

Will admitted that he usually had a hard time convincing clients to release fish. Some of the people got downright hostile, calling him nasty things like—well, like a yobbo, for instance. Mysteriously, people on Will's trips who released fish invariably wound up seeing lies and backwaters that others didn't. Funny how that happens. I often heard Wayne talk about getting into the guiding business as well, but one of his biggest concerns was that if he guided Aussies half his clients would return to the same spot the next day with their buddies and haul the fish out. He was serious when he said this, with a grave look on his face.

Although I wouldn't arrive there for a couple of weeks, I found out in short order that things aren't much better in Tasmania, Australia's southernmost island state. I met a lot of locals there who boasted about their flyfishing skills, waving a sacrosanct Sage rod in one hand and a stringer of trout in the other. I remember the first time I visited Bronte Lagoon, one of the better-known fishing spots in Tasmania's moorish Central Highlands. The driver I'd hitched a ride with dropped me off where the gravel road abutted a small group of fishing shacks along the lagoon's west shore. The first thing I noticed, hanging from a wooden porch rafter in the bronze flush of early morning, were a half-dozen brown trout. One of the shack's occupants told me that he and a couple of mates from a fishing club in Hobart, the state capital, had caught the fish at sunrise. They weren't planning to eat the trout themselves, he said, but to take them back to the city to distribute amongst their friends.

Over the next couple of days, I often fished along the same bank as one of the club members. I never saw one put a fish back. Thankfully, the fishing was tough, and they didn't take more than one or two each per day. But these were wild, self-sustaining stock, and it broke my heart each and every time I saw an angler stuff one into a creel.

Still, there was hope, literally, on the horizon. The plane loads of foreign anglers who had started to descend on Tasmania in increasing numbers were packing a lot more than fly rods and waders. They were also bringing a new attitude to Down Under fishing, which said that you didn't have to club a fish over the head to crown a successful outing.

The Tasmanian fishing regulations reflected an increasingly conservationist bent as well. Natural bait was prohibited on many lakes and lagoons, the use of motorized boats was often restricted, and some watersheds, such as renowned Little Pine Lagoon, were reserved for flyfishing only. Like anywhere else, the anglers themselves had initiated many of the changes after watching the angling quality steadily deteriorate over the years. When you begin hearing eighteen-year-olds talking about the "old days," you know it's time to do something and do it quick.

From Lake Eucumbene and the Murrumbidgee River area north of the town of Adaminaby, I worked my way east and north, eventually winding up at Canberra, the national capital. Selected in 1908 as a diplomatically neutral site between rival cities Sydney and Melbourne, Canberra was actually designed by an American architect, Walter Burley Griffin. The city is pretty enough, with a large man-made lake and plenty of parks with rolling green lawns, but nevertheless I found it rather sterile and stuffy, as national capitals are wont to be. With just over 200,000 people, Canberra supposedly derived its name from an Aboriginal term meaning "meeting place."

Appropriately, I'd arranged by telephone to meet a fellow at a small flyfishing shop there to pick up a new rod I'd had them set aside. It was another four-piece, nine-foot six-weight, cost $300 (American), was built from New Zealand-made Graphite III blanks, and slipped into my Sage tube to replace the broken rod I'd long since orphaned. Before I had time to even try out the new rod, I was leaving Canberra on a bus back to Melbourne to make my flight to Tasmania.

It began to dawn on me that everyday logistics were playing a larger role in my trip than I'd planned. I was spending far too much time on buses, in hostels, and dashing through airports like O. J. Simpson but with a pack on my back. I hoped the confines of Tasmania would give me more time for fishing.

The island of Tasmania isn't the sort of fishing destination you point your finger to on a map and say, "I'm going there." It's more likely that while you're holding your finger on, say, New Zealand or Chile, you excitedly spit a crumb, go to sweep it off the page and notice that, by golly, there's land *under* that speck of carrot cake! It gets you to thinking, "Well, geez, since I'm going to be over there anyway . . . "

Officially, Tasmania is an Australian state. Don't buy that. Tasmania has as much in common with Oz as Hawaii does with America. It's a colonial grab bag, something that's left over and you don't quite need yourself, but be damned if anyone else is going to get it, either.

Anyway, in the case of Tasmania, situated at the same latitude south of the equator as Wyoming is to the north, it turned out to be a handy place for the British to ship nineteenth-century convicts. Surrounded by turbulent, shark-infested seas, it had many of the same qualities as the American island prison of Alcatraz, only on a much larger scale. Back then Tasmania was dubbed "that isthmus between earth and hell," a heart-shaped island lying about 150 miles south of mainland Australia and north of Antarctica. The Tasmanian archipelago is actually an extension of the Great Dividing Range, which runs north for thousands of miles along the continent's east coast, includes the Snowy Mountains, and parallels the Great Barrier Reef along most of the coastline of the state of Queensland.

Transportation to the penal colonies was abolished in 1856, and twenty years later, the last Tasmanian Aborigine died after Europeans had killed nearly four thousand in the first thirty-five years of white settlement. All in all, it's a tainted history that many people living there now would like to sweep under the carpet. That would be a mistake, however, because the history fits Tasmania like a noose. This is a cold, moorish, werewolf-sort-of-place. Hell, sometimes it's downright creepy, conjuring images of Heathcliff tossing bones to The Hound of the Baskervilles.

But Tasmania is also warm, snug, and inviting. The island residents, or Tassies, still have an insular diffidence about them that I found far more appealing than offensive. A Tassie's shell may be hard to crack, but if and when you accomplish the feat, that person will reach out and attach himself or herself to you like a tippet to a leader. It's a bond that has been largely forgotten back home, where distrust and motive erect barriers that no measure of familiarity can topple.

FISH TAILS

I would be tempted to call it the Lady of the Lake, but this was a man, on shore, holding a fishing rod in his hand, not Excalibur. It was just after dawn when he appeared out of the mist like an apparition, tipped his English driving cap to me, and introduced himself as Mr. So-and-So, at your service. That's what he said. No kidding. AT YOUR SERVICE!

You'll forgive me if I didn't catch the name, but AT YOUR SERVICE tends to throw you off a bit. A gray mist spiraled off Tasmania's Bronte Lagoon, the rising sun hurling splotches of amber against the bleak mosaic. Mr. So-and-So, nattily attired in an olive-drab, military-like fishing ensemble, looked as if he'd fallen from the pages of Izaak Walton.

"I'm writing a book," he said. I swear, that's the *very next thing* he said. I'M WRITING A BOOK.

"Oh," I said.

"It's about flyfishing around the world," he said. "I'm a Brit, and that's what I'm doing—flyfishing around the world."

I didn't know how to respond. I made small talk about the fishing. Nothing earthshaking. Mr. So-and-So said he had to be moving on. To New Zealand? To Argentina? No, apparently just farther up the shoreline. I watched him for awhile; watched him until he vanished into the mist as mysteriously as he had appeared. He hooked a dandelion but no trout. I wandered back up to my campsite to put the coffee on, shaking my head.

In Tasmania there are great rivers to fish for trout, rivers with their own histories, like the Esk, the Meander, and the Liffey. But it's the still-water fishing that makes Tasmania stand out, and nowhere is the still-water fishing better than in the Central Highlands, a series of elevated, marshy plateaus situated near the geographic center of the island. Here more than four thousand lakes, tarns, and lagoons dot the somber land-scape, almost all of them shallow and containing wild brown trout. Rainbow trout are present as well, but just as you go to Tasmania to fish stillwater over moving water, *Salmo trutta* is the fish of choice.

If this sounds inviting, wait, it gets better. Because Tasmania has the largest hydroelectric power system in Australia and generates about ten percent of the continent's total electricity, the Central Highlands are crisscrossed by aqueducts, canals, and wooden penstocks. What this means to the angler is that water levels fluctuate several yards from week to week and month to month—a variance that equates to considerable distances across the flat shores. For instance, I returned to Bronte Lagoon several times during the month I spent in Tasmania, and each time it looked like a different body of water.

The fish pick up on this, too. In the spring, from, say, late August to October, they're liable to follow the rising water right into the flooded tussocks to feed on spawning frogs. Later in the year the water is generally lower, but periodic flooding often lures trout into the grassy shores to rummage for worms, grubs, caterpillars, and spiders. The process is a bit like pelagic fish following an incoming tide onto the flats, and seeing a twenty-inch brown trout rooting around in six inches of water, its tail and dorsal fin protruding like a shark's, adds even further to the analogy.

In addition to fishing for tailing trout, Tasmania is also renowned for its "polaroiding." An effective stillwater technique, the best way to polaroid a lake is to get in, walk stooped through the shallows, and care-fully scan the water ahead of you from side to side. Because the trout are easiest to spot along a pale, silt-sand bed, it's a lot like wading the saltwater flats for bonefish.

This is as challenging as flyfishing gets. Spotting a fish is only the beginning. Unlike in a river, where even the smoothest current still has minor blemishes that can mask an errant cast, the surface of a calm lake is unforgiving. Slap the line on the water, coil the leader, line the fish—do any of these things and it's game over. For obvious reasons, the best polaroiding occurs when there's just enough wind to disturb the water and not enough to make spotting fish impossible. While a dry fly cast in front of a cruising trout will occasionally entice a strike, the best bet is to drop a small nymph in the trout's path, give it a twitch or two, and pray. More often than not the fish will swim on by and leave you shaking your head and second-guessing, but that's the sort of thing that, as someone who flyfishes, keeps you coming back again and again. Rejection may not sit well at a high school dance; to an angler, of course, it's an aphrodisiac and the next best thing to a fish on the line.

Bronte Lagoon epitomizes all that the Central Highlands have to offer. About a two-hour drive from the state capitol building in Hobart, a colorful, colonial city backed by mountains rising sharply out of Tasmania's southeast coastline, the lagoon is visible from the Lyell Highway between Tarraleah and Derwent Bridge. The Surveyors Monument where the highway crosses Bronte Canal marks the geographic center of Tasmania. For the most part, Bronte's shorelines are exposed and grassy, the only buildings around the lagoon consisting of a cluster of dilapidated angler's shacks on the sheltered west side. Flyfishers have plied the lagoon's waters since its creation in 1953, and as might be expected, every tuck and fold along the shoreline has a name: The "Fence Shore" abuts "Fly Corner," "Fly Corner" abuts the "Long Shore," the "Long Shore" abuts—well, anyway, you get the idea.

There were some great spots to pitch a tent a few hundred yards above Fly Corner where the grassy slope abruptly met a towering eucalyptus forest. This is where I camped. A number of those trees overlooking the exposed marshy flats were gutted and charred from lightning strikes, but surprisingly, many of them still stood. Game trails radiated outward through the lush green, waist-high ferns into the forest. At dusk, just after I had crawled into my one-man tent for the night, it wasn't unusual for Bennett's wallabies, which resemble miniature kangaroos, to emerge from the trees with a *thump, thump, thump* on their way to the flats to feed on the grasses there. I half-expected to wake up one night with a large foot through the side of my tent, but it never happened.

The afternoon I arrived at the lagoon was sunny and, mistakenly, I decided to set up camp before rigging up to fish. That's not to say I didn't check the water out first (what angler wouldn't have?) and, dumping my backpack, I scrambled down to the shore at Fly Corner. With the exception of the odd tuft of marsh grass sprouting from the water, the small bay looked featureless. But the water was clear and, slipping my Polaroids on and forcing myself to look *through* the surface to the bottom, I immediately noticed a series of submerged troughs and ditches running from the shoreline out into the lagoon.

There were trout in these depressions; I knew that because it wasn't long before they started rising to take mayfly duns hatching on the surface. I hurried back to pitch the tent and assemble the new fly rod I'd picked up in Canberra. I rigged up as fast as possible, but by the time I reached the lagoon again it was clouding over, the wind was picking up, and the fish had stopped rising. I tried various techniques without success. An hour or so later it was pouring and, with lightning bolts about, I headed for shelter.

Now, in the Canadian Rockies, an afternoon thundershower generally lasts an hour or two and that's it. Not so in Tasmania, where a forecast afternoon thundershower starts on a Thursday after lunch and lets up on Saturday. For the next three days, the sky flip-flopped between various shades of gray and black, and while a flyfisher's definition of bad weather can differ dramatically from the average person's, there was often lightning about, and I didn't want to end up like one of those trees next to my campsite.

So I stole time. When things looked safe, I slithered out of my tent like a snake, grabbed my rod, and headed for the lagoon. When things didn't look safe, I retreated up the bank. By the second morning, I still hadn't caught a fish but, by carefully watching a few flyfishers who *had,* sensed that I was on the verge of a great breakthrough.

The trick, I observed, was to dress in chive-green clothes like a tuft of grass, move like a heron, and cast like Lefty Kreh. The first two I

managed well enough; the third gave me some difficulty. The brown
trout tailing along Long Shore weren't making things any easier. They
usually appeared out of nowhere, tracing elaborate patterns in the
shallow water with their tails and dorsals while the nearest flyfisher,
doubled-over and, gingerly lifting one leg and then the other, stealth-
ily attempted to close the distance between himself and a fish.

Sometimes I think the trout were just having fun out there. Dis-
cretely spaced about fifty yards apart along the half-mile of shoreline,
they'd dip and dart and dally with no apparent method to their mad-
ness at all except to frustrate the pursuing anglers. When someone
finally did work in close enough for a cast, more often than not the fish
would either ignore him altogether or leave a pronounced V-wake
radiating across the surface as it headed for deeper water.

Some anglers were using tiny nymphs and others tiny dry flies. It
didn't seem to matter much either way. The only things consistently
being hooked were the bright yellow Tassie dandelions extending well
out into the water, and the same tufts of grass other flyfishers were trying to hide behind. In fact, the only anglers getting any action at all
didn't seem to do *anything* except stand motionless with their fly lines
dangling heedlessly on the water.

And then it hit me. Rather than going to the fish, these anglers were
letting the fish come to *them*. Experience had taught them that while
the brown trout's movements seemed random to the neophyte, the fish
actually patrolled beats as well defined as any policeman's during their
travels up and down the shoreline. Retreating to dry land, I started
from scratch and tied on a new fifteen-foot leader with a 5x tippet. To
the end of this I attached a size 20 black gnat, rubbed it with a bit of
floatant, and waded back into the lagoon.

Spotting a tailing fish, I dropped to my knees supplicant-style in
the shallow water and raised my rod to the heavens. Inching forward,
I tried shielding myself from the trout behind a prominent knot of
grass. Just as I got close enough to drop a fly behind the tussock, the
wind came up, the fish disappeared, and I had every reason to believe
that I'd been foiled once again. Still, I hadn't seen the tell-tale
"V" indicating the fish had bolted, so I figured what the hell, and
cast anyway.

The small fly slowly drifted about a dozen feet beyond and to the left of the grass clump. My thumb twitched on the cork grip. I stared at the fly so hard I thought it might sink. Time passed—five minutes? ten?—and still I left the fly on the water. The leader had gone taut by now and the stationary fly was bobbing on the wavelets. It looked ridiculous. I pictured the fish laughing at me.

It took the fly instead—snatched it from the surface of the water so abruptly that I subconsciously set the hook while my consciousness played catch-up. The shallow water erupted in a geyser-like boil, and the twenty-one-inch hen brown made two strong runs before I reached over my shoulder and realized that I'd forgotten my net on the shore. No matter. I worked the fish in tight, seized it with both hands—my rod flopping carelessly aside—and carried it to shore like a baby. Despite being blinded by the flash on my camera at least half-a-dozen times, it managed to swim off in the right direction.

That was the only trout I caught that day. I tried playing my little wading game on a few other fish, but the rain returned, and before long it was next to impossible to spot the cruising tails. It finally cleared again just before dark, and I wandered back down to the lagoon. There was nothing showing so I waded out and cast blindly, my only company a flooded upright dead tree sticking grotesquely out of the water that I first mistook for another angler.

It was quite peaceful until the kookaburras started laughing at me. The kookaburra is an Australian bird that looks a bit like a woodpecker, feeds on snakes and lizards, and has a twenty-second-long call best described as mad, hysterical laughter that will make the hair stand up on the back of your neck. *Hohohoho, hahahaha,* they shriek, usually at dusk, and the wail echoes across the marshes like a marauding band of lunatics. Unnerved, I went to bed.

The first thing I saw when I awoke the next morning was a brown leech descending end-over-end like a Slinky down the inside of the screen on my tent. I rolled over, tore a page from *The Caine Mutiny* and dispatched it, crushing it between the prose. After checking for holes and tears, I figured it must have found the tiny spot where the two zippers came together on the fly—something countless mosquitoes had failed to do. I'd heard of leeches gaining access to a foot through a boot-lace hole, but this was too much. I'd obviously overstayed my welcome. I broke camp and left.

A couple of days later the weather was still the pits, but there was reason to be optimistic. Or so said Martin, son of Denis and Robin Wiss, the amiable, middle-aged owners of Bronte Park Highland Village. Martin is a pony-tailed surfer and part-time bartender who follows the weather with keen interest. He's high during the highs and low during the lows, and at that moment he was pouring me ten ounces of Boag's draft from the spigot behind the bar.

"What's the story?" I asked him.

"Well," he said, "it looks like this." Grabbing the nearest bar napkin, he deftly drew me a detailed weather map the likes of which would make a newspaper proud. There were highs and lows and troughs and fronts, but the bottom line was that nice weather was on the way.

"Cheers," I said, tipping my mug.

"Cheers," he replied.

After being cooped up in my tent for a couple of days, the village was a welcome respite. Originally built to house workers on the nearby hydroelectric projects, it now caters to tourists, offering accommodation in a central chalet, a series of self-contained cottages, a hostel, and a caravan. I was staying in the hostel, which previously served as the village hospital.

It had a do-it-yourself kitchen, a large games room with a black pot-bellied stove in the corner, and a number of bunk rooms varying from cramped to crowded. Fortunately, because there were only a handful of us staying there at any one time, I usually had a room to myself.

The village is a favored stopover for anglers. During my first week there I threw back the curtains one morning and two elderly gents, one smoking a pipe, were casting fly lines on the grass in front of a cottage. It was cool then, and the cottage chimneys issued gray strands of smoke that drifted over the pink and blue and purple fields of lupine wildflowers. A white-backed magpie, commonly called a piping crow-shrike in Oz and differing from a North American magpie in that the whites and blacks are arranged differently on the bird, watched intently from a post, no doubt wondering what on earth those two fellows were up to.

I walked down to the small general store to pick up some groceries for my next fishing trip. The potatoes in the bin were so dirty that half the farmer's field must have been pulled out with them. The bread was in the freezer to keep until the next delivery, which couldn't have been far off because half the shelves were empty. I did manage to find some important outdoor necessities, however—things like hair conditioner and cling-free dryer pads.

Up at the chalet the dining room wasn't quite ready to start serving lunch, so I wandered over to one of the couches facing the stone fireplace and leafed through *Trout Days*, a book by Australian flyfishing author David Scholes. Denis came over with a footstool-sized log and tossed it on the fire.

"How's the fishing been going ?" he asked.

"So-so," I said. "It's tougher than I thought it would be."

We made small talk for a couple of minutes, and he left to attend to some chores. The log smoldered in the fire but didn't catch. The room was empty, and I leaned my head back against the couch. Homesickness welled up in my throat, but I fought it off. I looked around the large dining room, admiring the woodwork, which reminded me of Wayne's flat back in Jindabyne. Then Becky came up and told me I could order lunch now if I wanted.

Becky was Martin's girlfriend, a sprite of a thing with laughing eyes and long, dark hair. I think she felt sorry for me, not understanding why anyone would want to travel halfway around the world to fish with flies. She always went out of her way to be friendly. I enjoyed her company, but was still smarting from an episode a couple of nights earlier in the pub. I'd ordered fish and chips and went to reach for the salt shaker. It was filled with rice.

"Excuse me," I asked Becky. "Do you think I could have another salt shaker? This one has rice in it." A handful of locals sitting at the bar chuckled and exchanged knowing glances. *Outsider.* They didn't need to say it.

"We put the rice in so the damp air won't cause the salt to clump up," Becky politely explained. She sensed my embarrassment. "But that one does look low on salt."

Since then she'd picked up on my weakness for sweets and had made a point of slipping me an extra silver-wrapped chocolate mint with my coffee after supper. "To make you strong for the fishing," she'd say, and we'd have a good laugh.

From the village I walked the four miles north to the rolling Nive River valley and Pine Tier Lagoon. Traffic was almost nonexistent on the gravel road, dusty despite the rainy weather of late. Cows munched contentedly as I passed. Small brooks, no more than trickles, really, meandered in and out of sight amongst the tall meadow grasses. More conspicuous was the concrete flume of the canal draining the lagoon, which carried as much water as a small river and wound incongruously through the thick eucalyptus forest. Despite the lagoon's name, I didn't see any pines, at least not the sort of pines I'm accustomed to seeing in the Rocky Mountains. The closest facsimiles were unfamiliar shrubs resembling overgrown junipers.

Actually, Pine Tier Lagoon was antithetical to Bronte Lagoon in almost every way. Excluding marshy Gowan Brae Bay at the mouth of the Pine River, the rest of the lagoon was bounded by eucalyptus and a gravelly shoreline that tumbled steeply into the water. But appearances can be deceiving. Pine Tier's eastern shore was a classic example of that. The clear water along the rocky shoreline was tangled with deadfall; mossy stumps and logs made perfect holding lies for trout. A couple of feet out, thick weed beds trailed vermilion and jade tendrils along a sharp drop-off. There wasn't a lot of space for a flyfisher to ply his craft, but it was possible.

I walked about a quarter of a mile down the shoreline from my campsite, where I'd been forced to pitch my tent on an incline just steep enough to guarantee insomnia. Still, it was the first sunny afternoon in a long time—Martin, the surfing meteorologist, had been right—and I was able to position myself so that I'd be fishing with my casting arm out over the water and a slight breeze quartering across my back. I couldn't have devised a better scenario. The brown trout weren't rising regularly, but every now and then a gust of wind would knock a few beetles out of the eucalyptus trees along the shore, and the fish rose to the occasion.

I tied on a size 12 Red Tag, a Down Under attractor pattern that's supposed to be a catch-all beetle imitation but honestly looks more like an oversized black midge with a tuft of red yarn sticking out in place of a tail. That didn't seem to bother the trout; they charged headlong to eat the thing. Once, when the fly hung up on some pin grass near the shore, a brown trout jumped clear out of the water to pluck it off the stem. I watched, stunned, as the trout hooked itself upon re-entry. It was just that kind of a day.

Beetle patterns are standard fare for the Down Under flyfisher, much more so than in western North America, where fly tiers generally limit their terrestrials to grasshoppers. Back home, I carry three or four hopper patterns in preparation for some great late-season terrestrial fishing on the Bow River and Alberta's prairie streams. I can't honestly say, however, that I'd ever used a beetle. I think I have a couple buried in a fly box somewhere, but I bought them years ago when I was just starting out. Stocking up on one or two drab-looking flies that worked didn't seem as exciting then as searching for a pot of gold at the end of a feathery rainbow. That said, any angler in Tasmania would do well to take along several green Gum Beetles, Black Beetles, Red Tags, and Coch-y-bondus in sizes 10 through 14. When the beetles start dropping out of shoreline eucalyptus trees on hot windy days, the fishing can get frantic.

Most of the fish I caught that afternoon were small by Tasmanian standards, somewhere in the ten- to fourteen-inch range. A couple were larger. One eighteen-inch beauty charged out from beneath an overhanging willow, excited beyond caution when it saw the fly plop on the water. I worked my way along the shore back to my campsite, then struggled back up and repeated the process all over again. It was one of the most memorable flyfishing afternoons I've ever had. I guess you could call it a divine gift, because the next day was Christmas.

Christmas Eve passed slowly, my thoughts filled with family and friends. I didn't feel sorry for myself, though, because I was living the life I had chosen. I consoled myself by noting that in North America, on the other side of the International Date Line, it was actually only December 23rd. Mom's turkey was still in the freezer. My supper in Tasmania? Sliced onion and potato boiled with chicken stock and two packets of chicken noodle soup. Filling and hearty but not quite the same. Besides, I'd run out of toilet paper that morning and would have traded half the afternoon's fish for a tissue or two.

On the day after Christmas I passed the afternoon in the Bronte Park pub. I felt like chatting with Martin, but his sister Allison said he'd gone surfing with Becky on the coast. A drunk "guide" was slobbering in my face and four anglers in neoprene chest waders talked excitedly at the next table. Two of the pairs of neoprene waders looked brand new; they must have been Christmas presents. From their accents I could tell that the four men were Tassies. They got up to shoot pool and still they left their waders on, suspenders hinged over their shoulders and sweat beading on their foreheads. The waders were like badges and they weren't about to take them off.

"What a bunch of jokers," the "guide" said a little too loudly. I thought there might be trouble, but the four fishermen were making too much noise to hear.

"Jokers!" the "guide" repeated, and his head slouched so far forward that I thought he was going to bang it on the table.

I decided to make another three-day trip to Bronte Lagoon. The water had dropped a couple of feet since the last time I'd been there, and the shoreline was almost unrecognizable. At least fifty yards of grass that had been underwater two weeks earlier was now high and dry. The tailing fish were nowhere to be seen.

As it turned out, they'd merely changed venues, moving over to where the Fence Shore abuts Fly Corner. The drop-off was more pronounced there, and the fish were gathering in pods and cruising up and down the shallows with the tenacity of a youth gang out for trouble. Venturing out into the knee-deep water, I found that if I stood absolutely still they'd actually swim right by me, passing within feet. Based on past experience, of course, I was shocked. The only logical explanation seemed to be that the trout, like the youth gang, found safety in numbers. That was fine by me. I liked the numbers, too.

At least one habit remained unchanged, however: the fish were still circling in well-defined beats. You can't really blame several nearby anglers for staring at me strangely when I cast *behind* a group of cruising fish, but I knew what I was doing. A minute later, the entire pod turned in unison and swam straight at me. The leading dimple snatched my fly from the surface.

This was a brown trout in name alone. It was sea-run silver, about seventeen inches, and the garish red spots with cream-colored halos were so pronounced that it looked like it had the measles. There were almost no black spots at all. Surprisingly, the pod resumed feeding unabated and I took two clones of the first trout before retiring to the bank for lunch.

Because the Christmas holidays were in full swing, there were more anglers around the lagoon than usual, many staying in the club shacks with their families. One of them walked up to me and asked how it was going. I told him and asked the same.

"I picked up one this morning and missed three this afternoon," he said. His green vest was full of patches that identified him as belonging to such-and-such a club and having fished at such-and-such a location. Pins and medals cluttered his hat. He tried to make it look like he wasn't checking out what fly I had attached to my hookkeeper, but I knew that he was.

It always amazed me how much emphasis Tasmanian anglers put on missed fish. I mean, let's face it, it's not something you go around boasting about in North America. On another trip, I met a local angler who proudly told me that his buddy had caught two fish that morning while he had "dropped three." In fairness, the fishing there *is* tough, and counting strikes and misses could be interpreted as an indication of that. Even at the region's most popular angling destinations, catch rates are surprisingly low. Two fish per angler per day is really good going; some of the best lagoons average half that. It's probably due to a combination of things, the two most obvious being the wildness of the brown trout and the difficulty of stalking them along the shallow shorelines. It wasn't long before I was counting the misses, too. After all, a person has to stay sane.

Speaking of sanity, the kookaburras were keeping me awake one night in my tent when I laughingly recalled a conversation with a friend back home. I was just starting to plan my trip, that crumb of carrot cake had fallen on Tasmania, and I'd mentioned to her that it would be a neat place to go. A couple of months later we had lunch just days before I left.

"I told my dad you were going to Tasmania," Shela said. "He said to watch out for the vampires."

It took a moment to sink in. "I think he meant Transylvania," I corrected. "That's in Rumania."

A kookaburra burst into fiendish laughter outside the tent. I thought back to my encounter with Mr. So-and-So, AT YOUR SERVICE! Come to think of it, I hadn't bothered to look for fangs. Maybe I should have.

A scruffy-looking Japanese fellow drives up on a motorcycle just after dinner. I'm staying at the hostel in Bronte Park. I've been here a week now, and he's the first Oriental I've seen. The man unloads a couple of panniers, a four-piece fly rod, and a box full of commercially tied flies. He speaks almost no English, myself, no Japanese. Between the two of us, we string together enough nouns and gestures to convey that he's from northern Japan and I'm from Canada.

"Tlout big," he says, holding his hands about twenty inches apart.

I can't figure out whether he's talking about Tasmania, Canada, or Japan.

"Where?" I ask. "Canada?"

He stares, slowly comprehending. "Japan," he says. "Tlout big."

"I didn't even know they had trout in Japan."

"Huh?"

We fall silent. A moment later he reaches into a pannier and pulls out a local fishing map.

"Where fish?" he asks, pointing at me and then at the map. I study it a moment, take his pencil, and draw a circle around the Long Shore at Bronte Lagoon. "Sank-you," he says, gathering up his things and rushing out the door. He's back an hour later. I gather that he discovered he couldn't ride his bike past the locked gate leading to Long Shore and didn't want to walk in. I get the point across that it doesn't matter, that the best fishing has been at dawn. Apparently, he doesn't like to fish in the morning.

"Like sleep," he says, grinning.

He points to several lakes on the map and shakes his head. "No like." I point to a river. He nods vigorously. Apparently, he likes rivers. If so, he's come to the wrong place, because Bronte Park is noted for its lagoon and lake fishing. Over the next half hour I manage to learn that he's here for a month's vacation. He fishes in Japan, but there are lots of flyfishers on even the remotest water. The average trout is small and hatchery raised.

We fall silent again. A moment later I reach for a ping-pong paddle and gesture towards the table. We try to play, but the only ball is cratered and we soon give up.

"Dlink?" he says, gripping his fist around the handle of an invisible mug and bringing it to his lips. "Beer?"

"Sure."

The pub is noisy and we sit at a small table. There is a large map of the world on a wall and I point to Calgary, my home in Canada. He points to a small town in northern Japan. I can't make out the name. We return to the table and clink our glasses.

"To trout," I say.

"To tlout."

LAST CHANCE TO TASMANIA

Standing in Idaho's Henry's Fork River next to Mike Lawson epitomizes intimidation. It's a bit like being paired with Jack Nicklaus at Augusta or making your Wimbledon debut and seeing Boris Becker across the net. Mike doesn't know me from a corky, but I know him. Some time ago, *Outside* magazine featured Mike in a splashy profile. The gist of the article was that Mike and the Henry's Fork have, over a number of years, become synonymous—sort of joined at the hip waders, if you will.

So, although I was a bit surprised when Mike emerged from a path in the forest and began fishing next to me in the Box Canyon, I was not shocked. He cast like I had imagined he would cast, with long, fluid loops that soared off the end of his rod like eagles off a cliff. I reeled in, found a level streamside rock, sat back, and watched.

The fishing was painfully slow. It was late June, and the dry Idaho heat had settled into Box Canyon and closed the lid on itself. It must have been ninety degrees. Across the river, a guide waded in water up to his chest and eased a McKenzie drift boat along the bank. His client slapped a dry salmonfly back and forth across the bow. Even from a distance, I could tell neither man was really into what he was doing. The fish weren't into anything.

"How's it goin'?" asked Mike, who had worked his way up to the pool below me, meticulously covering all the water with his effortless rhythm.

"It isn't."

Mike said he hadn't had much luck either, reeled in, and leap-frogged around me to continue fishing upstream. If Mike Lawson's getting shut down on the Henry's Fork, I thought to myself, then it's time to pack it in. Problem was, I was floating alone in my Metzeler inflatable raft, and my truck was waiting several hours downstream outside Mike's shop at the town of Last Chance. Years ago, when friends started getting married and regular fishing partners fell by the wayside, I began searching for ways to optimize my solo fishing trips. On Montana's Bighorn River one afternoon, I'd met two fellows from Idaho who were using one-man inflatable kayaks to make their way down the river. They spoke enthusiastically and it seemed like a pretty good idea, so I started shopping around back in Calgary.

That's when I found the Metzeler, which is basically a dwarfish version of your typical Avon fishing raft. The Metzeler is actually designed as a tender to be towed behind a yacht, but I find it ideal for floating rivers where vehicle shuttles are available. The only drawback is that I can't fish from the boat unless I want to drop an anchor or take a Huck Finn approach and brace the rod between my legs through slow-water stretches. I prefer to get out and wade.

As I drifted along the Henry's Fork in my raft, poking an oar in every now and then to avoid broaching on a boulder, the heat penetrated my mind and I fell into a dazed reverie. I'd always dreamed of fishing the Henry's Fork, and here I was, but somehow the dream was not living up to its advance billing. And it wasn't just that particular afternoon, either, because the day before I'd overheard an old-timer complaining about the fishing. In fact, even the local media was dumping on the Henry's Fork, a brash act verging on sacrilege.

Naturally, I asked myself the only logical question: "What am I doing here?" When I failed to come up with a reasonable response, I then asked myself, "And if this is the most hallowed river in fishing-dom, what's left?"

I thought about that for awhile, and my mind drifted, and before you know it my mind had drifted clear across the Pacific Ocean and run aground on Tasmania. T-A-S-M-A-N-I-A. It had a nice sound to it. I'd seen it in an atlas—dropped that crumb of carrot cake and read about Tasmania in a magazine—and it had a nice look to it, too. The fishing there was supposed to be good, and even if it wasn't, I'd be too far removed to worry about having to answer to family and friends. A clear conscience, a clean getaway. What could be better?

I'd take a sabbatical. Store my stuff. Frankly, I was at a stage in my life where I needed a great getaway. My thirtieth birthday was approaching, life at the newspaper was getting routine, and that ever-elusive girlfriend who could curb my wanderlust had failed to materialize. Most of my friends had been on a prolonged trip or two, and I figured it was my turn. Besides, what better excuse to get a dose of "culture" and fish myself into the ground at the same time? I'd seen a documentary on TV about a group of surfers who had set off around the world in search of the perfect wave. Well, when the time came to explain things, I'd just say that I was in search of the perfect trout. I thought of all those things and more as I floated down the Henry's Fork, and by the time I reached my truck and beached the raft, I'd made up my mind. Last Chance to Tasmania. A year later I was on the plane.

As you've probably gathered by now, Tasmania continues to gnaw at my memory like a beaver on a poplar. I can't shake it. I'm not sure I want to. I think what drew me to Tasmania is the general perception that it's one of trout fishing's final frontiers. There are still places in Tasmania where, without resorting to an airplane or helicopter, an angler can fish all day without seeing another person. Not just another angler—another *person.* Something about that appeals to the hermit in me.

The highlight of any Tasmanian fishing trip is a bushwalk into the Western Lakes, the land that time forgot. You won't find them on a map (at least not under that name), but mention to any Tassie that you're heading into the Western Lakes, and he or she will nod knowingly, giving you the same suspect look Columbus must have received before casting off.

The Western Lakes sit on an elevated plateau between Great Lake, Lake St. Clair, and the Mersey valley, but they might as well sit on another planet. There are actually hundreds of lakes and tarns in the system; most named, some not. The westernmost Western Lakes lie in the Walls of Jerusalem National Park, the remainder in a protected conservation area. As a result, the self-sustaining, wild brown trout that have inhabited the region since 1893 have been given a very good chance to celebrate a second centennial in 2093. Rainbows weren't introduced until 1940, but the upstarts have successfully populated several of the region's lakes and rivers. Nonetheless, this is primarily brown trout country, and that's what draws anglers from around the world to pit their skills against the world's wariest fish.

Of this there can be no argument: despite the healthy trout stocks, surveys show the catch rate in the Western Lakes is less than one trout per angler per day, or, if you'd rather, 7.4 hours of fishing per trout. I've fished the spring creeks of Montana, and those are smart fish, but they're not as smart as the Western Lakes' browns.

I might have missed out on the Western Lakes entirely if it hadn't been for Colin. A laborer from Melbourne, I met him at the Bronte Park hostel one morning, and we were fishing together within the hour. His employment on the mainland was seasonal, so in the summer he'd pick up, move to Tasmania, and fish and bushwalk for several months on end. Because he also occasionally led bushwalking tours into the remote moorland and rainforests, Colin knew the state intimately. A delight to fish with, he often kidded me about my expensive gear, boasting that his two glass rods averaged $20 apiece, and his plastic reel was held together with Crazy Glue.

With reddish hair and a neatly trimmed moustache and beard, Colin perfectly fit the adventurer stereotype. Guessing him to be in his mid- to late thirties, he had a triathlete's build and the restlessness of an eight-inch brookie. Even during the slowest fishing, however, he persevered, trying every fly in his box and every trick in his arsenal.

"Just one more cast," was more than an expression to him, it was a way of life.

Colin proposed the Western Lakes trip just after New Year's. Without a vehicle, fishing in the area was an impossible proposition, because it took a good bit of rough-road driving just to reach the trailhead at the first major lake, Augusta. Colin's white '71 Mercedes was not in the best condition, but it did its job, getting us the twenty-odd miles from Miena, on the south shore of Great Lakes, to the southeast shore of Lake Ada, and the start of the bushwalk.

After divvying up a week's worth of tucker, or food, Colin and I set off along a unused cart track northwest toward Lake Fanny and the Powena Creek drainage. The terrain was open, relatively flat, wet, and rocky. It reminded me of something the *Star Trek* producers might have come up with for Kirk, Spock, and Bones to trudge through on yet another weekly misadventure. Even the soil between the clumps of snowgrass and boulders overgrown with moss was Martian red. Truth was, I half-expected to stumble across an alien around each bend.

The bushwalk covered only six miles but took over three hours. When we got to Lake Fanny, shaped like a shark's tooth and a little under a mile long, the trail ended and the real fun began. We were headed to the far corner, Colin explained, his head bobbing in and out of view as we wove through the brush along the quaggy east shore. The west shore was sheltered by a prominent rock tier covered by gnarled, half-dead eucalyptus. A damp mist had rolled up the valley and it started to drizzle.

"This looks like a good spot to pitch our tents," Colin said.

"*Here?*" Taking a look around, I got the feeling a wrong step in any direction would lead to my demise. The peat beneath our boots was wet and spongy, a sickly yellow and green color that reminded me of bile and vomit. And because the sloping bank dropped steadily down to the lake shore, familiar thoughts of a tilted sleeping bag and sleepless nights popped into my mind like rivets.

"Well, it's as flat as we're going to find, and now it looks like the weather's turning crook," Colin said.

Fact was, he had a point. We each managed to find a moderately level spot and scrambled to get our tents up before the rain came in earnest. It let up within minutes, the sky cleared, and Colin wandered off with his fly rod to do some prospecting along the lake shore. I passed, choosing instead to sleep off the effects of the bushwalk before supper.

Colin and I spent about an hour that evening casting flies in a secluded bay near the campsite. Hopping from rock to rock until I'd reached a promontory well out into the clear water, I tied on a size 10 green Flashback and cast about seventy feet of floating line, letting the leader sink for a few seconds before starting the retrieve. The first take was instant and unexpected. Deceived but not to be outdone, the brown trout rolled on the surface and sent the nymph springing back at me through the air. "There, take *that*!"

Gathering my line and my composure, I tried again. Nothing doing. Is it just me, or do other anglers often hook a fish right off the bat, then inevitably slowly coast down the plane of expectation, finally bottoming out with dashed hopes and cold hands? If it was any consolation, Colin didn't even get a bump.

The bad weather returned later that night; it was sleeting by the time we let the fire burn down and took our last leaks before turning in. The only sounds were the sleet pattering against the nylon tent and Colin tossing in his sleeping bag about ten yards away. By morning the precipitation had stopped. A gray mist swept across the lake and through the forest, smudging the distant trees and throwing them in and out of focus. It was eerier than hell, and Colin and I tilted our palms against the fire and let the warmth creep up our arms and into our chests. Only then did we reach for the cereal and our bowls and spoons. After breakfast and hot tea we started rigging up, tossing everything we wouldn't need that day into the tents. The morning sun hung like a silver coin in the thinning fog; before long, streaks of blue appeared and slowly gained hold. By the time we started hiking up Powena Creek, the mist had burned off and the sky was cloudless.

Once again, it was tough going. There was no trail and each step was an adventure. The trees thinned out then disappeared, giving way to patchy scrub and clumps of pastel-colored heath. As we advanced up the prehistoric-looking valley, the boulders grew progressively bigger, abandoned sentries left behind by the receding ice sheet during the last glaciation. Strangely out of place were the sporadic mounds of cushion plants, which resembled neon green velvet ottomans and yielded to a prodding finger like freshly baked bread. I tried not to step on them because I got the feeling the boot prints would have taken about half a million years to disappear.

"You know," I told Colin, staring at his back and the floppy camouflage hat perched atop his head, "instead of a fly rod I feel like I should be carrying a spear and wearing animal skins."

Powena Creek divided, then divided again; soon it became little more than countless trickles connecting a scattered series of small lakes, ponds, and lagoons. Colin said that during the spring floods, at high water, the trout were often flushed from one catchment to the next. That was why most if not all of them held fish. But some of the ponds were so isolated that they were only affected by severe flooding every ten or twenty years. Those were the ones to look for, Colin continued, because the living interment enabled the dislodged trout to attain immense proportions—anywhere from five pounds up. As I'd soon find out, spotting a trout that size in a shallow pond no larger than a swimming pool was a lot like staring at a goldfish through the side of an aquarium.

Eventually we decided to split up, Colin setting off along one side of the ill-defined valley and myself the other. I had no idea where to start fishing. Each new hillock revealed dozens of tiny ponds. Deciding to approach a network of three or four through waist-high brush, I scared the hell out of myself when a small brown wallaby burst from cover not ten feet away. There was another, then another . . . within seconds they erupted over the entire hillside like a covey of flushed partridge. Stopping for a moment to catch my breath, I noticed a rise against the far shore of the nearest pond. A few seconds later the fish rose again, a dainty, sipping action generally indicative of a good trout. Stooping low to avoid detection, I crept along the bankside scrub to get within range.

Two or three good false casts put the size 14 Adams exactly where I wanted it, the leader unfurling as the plan unfolded. The 5x tippet caused almost no disturbance. I waited. And waited. And then, about twenty feet farther up the same shoreline, another trout rose. (Who knows, could it have been the same trout?) Ducking low, I continued up the shoreline, hoping to actually spot the trout, but thwarted by a frustrating surface glare. The fish seemed to be holding steady, so once again, keeping my rod high to avoid tangling in the brush, I made a nice cast from a crouch. And, once again, the trout shut down. When another trout started rising, I switched to 6x and a smaller fly. Still no luck. I tried drawing a tiny nymph across the pond—even let a midge pupae dangle beneath a motionless indicator. All the usual spooky-lake tricks. Nothing doing.

It got so tense I wanted to jump in the water and thrash, splashing and hollering and letting every trout in range know that "yes, I'm here you little bastards, and now we all damn-well know it!" Just then, my crazed stare was distracted by a palm-sized green skink slithering across a boulder. It halted in the sun and twitched its tail. "I wonder . . .," I began, remembering lobbing grasshoppers into the creeks back home and watching them vanish in a slurping moil. The lizard twitched again. I lunged. Came up empty. Oh, my God, is this what it's come to?

That afternoon the weather changed abruptly, something I soon got used to in Tasmania, especially after hanging around Martin, the surfing meteorologist. Coming from the Canadian Rockies, of course, I'd grown up with my share of changeable weather. The wind picked up, blowing out of the southeast, then the clouds started rolling in, straight from the *northwest.* Only in Tasmania, I thought. But the chop on the water was the break I'd been looking for. Stray caddis began dipping onto the wavelets, and the trout took notice. I was fishing on a steep-sided pond about the size of a small backyard. A few fish were grouped around the inlet where the creek was flushing caddis into their waiting mouths. It was impossible to cast from the overgrown bank—impossible to *walk*—so I eased along in the water and straddled the branches drooping into the pond, staying as close to shore as possible and terrified that each footfall would panic the trout.

On the first cast I hooked my shirt-sleeve, which struggled admirably as I tried to yank the hook back through the fabric. On the second cast I hooked a thirteen-inch brown, which grabbed the size 14 Elk Hair Caddis and headed straight for a tangle. I turned the fish before things got ugly, and it fought well before I reached down to pluck the fake from its jaw.

On the next pond down the creek drainage, I got another hit but missed, swearing in unison to a crack of thunder over the ridge. The sky was turning black, the temperature plummeting. Despite the temptation to fish on, I decided to pack it in. I've always had this nagging fear of getting roasted alive on a graphite spit. It was starting to rain by the time I arrived back at camp. Colin wandered in about twenty minutes later, soaked and toting a nice fourteen-inch brown that he'd decided to keep for supper.

The drizzle persisted through the evening, then turned to sleet, mirroring the weather of the night before. It was hard to believe that that afternoon there'd been lizards crawling on the rocks. Colin cooked the fish by wrapping it in foil with several slabs of garlic butter: five minutes a side, buried under the embers, then our fingers burning trying to tear open the foil because we couldn't wait to taste the moist orange flesh.

"Man, does that ever hit the spot," I said, water dripping off my jacket hood and popping in the fire.

"Bloody right," Colin replied.

The next morning it was foggy again, then it cleared, and we were off up the valley in a repeat of the day before. Colin caught a fish before we split up—a blunt-nosed brown he outwitted by throwing a dry fly on the water and waiting a good five minutes before it happened along. Hoisting the trout onto the shore crane style (it was a miracle the leader didn't break), he muttered, "Beautiful, beautiful," then thumped it on the head in preparation for that night's supper. Tinfoiled again.

Later that morning, I hooked and lost another small brown, but the day's highlight was stumbling upon two big browns in a shallow lagoon with a beige, silt-covered bottom. It was the sort of impoundment Colin had talked about the day before, the jumbo trout destined to spend the rest of their lives there. My objective, of course, was to toss them a fly or two and give at least one of them a little anxiety in an otherwise unhurried existence.

At least that was the plan. A quick perusal of the surrounding shoreline showed why the pair had grown so large. There was no cover. Nothing. Just a bowl-shaped amphitheater with me peeking over the edge and thinking that sneaking up on a gull in the middle of Dodger Stadium would have been easier. Slithering down the slope on elbows and knees like an assault soldier, I got to the edge of the water and tried hiding behind a rock I'd hesitate to call a boulder. One of the trout, the smaller of the pair (it was still at least three pounds), came cruising by, swimming laps around the lagoon the same way a captive lion paces back and forth behind the bars. I froze, following it with my eyes in duck-hunter fashion. Before it circled again, I pulled the leader and a few feet of line through the guides. It would be reaching to call what followed a cast, but keeping the rod tip back from the water, I managed to flick a dry fly out far enough that the trout would intercept it on the next pass.

I waited fifteen minutes, maybe twenty, periodically flipping the leader over to take the kinks out. Because I was so close to the surface of the water, spotting the fish was impossible. I just had to wait and hope. Finally a trout—it looked like the smaller of the two again—came cruising around the bend. It saw my fly, and swam over to inspect it. I felt detached, as if my eye had become a camera lens filming a segment for an upcoming fishing show. Then I made a fatal mistake. Anxious that the fish was taking too long to make up its mind, I twitched the fly, hoping to entice a strike. The effect couldn't have been more opposite. The trout fled across the pond, no doubt spooking its larger brethren en route. When I crawled back up to higher ground to reinspect the water, there was no sign of either fish.

Following another day at Powena Creek and two more a short bushwalk away at Silver Lake and its environs, my Western Lakes batting average was just that—average. Slightly less than a fish a day, or if you'd rather, too many hours spent catching too few trout. Colin was faring marginally better, but all things considered, his tinfoil was in no danger of running out. Looking back now, it's clear that slowly, unwittingly, a friction borne of frustration and a sense of competition had begun to chafe at us. Long spells of silence around the campfire were interrupted by sarcastic remarks, caveman-like grunts. Techniques were questioned, egos bruised.

"It probably wouldn't hurt to cut down on your false casting," I said.

"How many fish did *you* catch today?"

The more we talked about fishing, the more we seemed to get on each other's nerves. Realizing what was happening but unable to stop it, the *really* frustrating part was that I'd never considered myself a competitive angler. In fact, I usually went out of my way to *avoid* counting fish. And yet I couldn't deny the way I was feeling, hauling the tension out onto the water with me each day, knowing that I'd kill every trout I landed just to one-up Colin. Wanting to fish with him because I liked his company; wanting to fish alone because I couldn't bear to see him catch another fish. Tasmania had slipped its noose around my neck. Hypocrisy was daring me to kick the chair out from underneath.

It was midday when we arrived at Christys Creek, the last stop of the trip. We were both anxious to start fishing, but Colin took the time to point out the largest ant I'd ever seen. "An inchman," he said, and the ant was, indeed, an inch long. Like a solitary hunter, it traveled alone. When I poked it with a twig, it reared like a grizzly, sniffing the air to catch my scent.

"You're lucky it's not a jackjumper," said Colin, suddenly brimming with information about the fierce Tasmanian ants, which made the ants back home look like—well, like smaller ants. "It would have sprung at you by now."

Christys Creek is similar to Powena Creek but not as isolated. The abandoned cart track is never far away. Of course, that doesn't mean much in Tasmania. The area still probably sees fewer anglers each year than some of the remotest Rocky Mountain lakes in the U.S. and Canada. Once again, as far as the fishing is concerned, the creek itself is ancillary to the tarns and lagoons studding its course.

Knowing that we only had one afternoon and evening left before bushwalking out the next morning, we hurriedly pitched our tents and rushed off in separate directions. *Gentlemen, start your engines . . .*

The wind was blowing, but there was no sign of the clouds that had been building each day. The first tarn I came across was surrounded by intermittent brush and exposed, rocky shore. It was only a couple of hundred yards across, the gusting wind sending kaleidoscopic patterns sweeping across the surface. During a lull, I noticed a line of riseforms along the windward bank. Circling the pond for a closer look revealed why. Every time the wind abated a swarm of black mayfly spinners left the shore-side brush and dropped onto the water. The trout, as anticipatory as school kids in a cafeteria line, eagerly awaited. The larger fish were porpoising, their broad gold backs glinting in the sun. The smaller fish made splashy rises: it was easy to distinguish the dolphins from the mackerel.

"Holy shit!" I said to myself, starved from too many lean days. "This is IT."

Concentrating on a particularly nice fish working about three feet from an overhanging bush, I eased into the water and positioned myself so that I'd be casting sideways to the wind. The idea was to throw just enough slack into the line so that the fly would drift naturally over the trout. Kneeling behind a rock outcrop, I watched the fish roll, timed the delay, and cast a size 10 Black Spinner. The trout rolled again on cue, eclipsing my fly.

It made a strong run for deeper water, then another, and then, after about ten minutes, I backed it up against the shore (I didn't have a net), and reached down to seize the twenty-inch fish between two boulders. Picking it up, I swirled towards dry land, fully intending to bash it on the head and take it back to camp to lay at Colin's feet. But the trout had other ideas. Perhaps sensing its imminent demise, it squirmed free, dropping into the water *sans* fly. It looked stunned, but when I reached down to grab it again, it darted away, carrying my bragging rights out into the middle of the pond.

I kicked the water, screaming obscenities. That's what it had come to. That's how low I'd fallen. Later that afternoon I caught another brown trout of equal size on the other side of the pond. I killed it, of course, throwing it on the bank and bashing it on the head with a blunt rock until the skin discolored and its eyes rolled back and filmed over.

I took it to Colin and laid it at his feet. He'd kept another trout about an inch smaller. That night, we decided to cook the larger of the two—*my* fish—and save the other one for breakfast. We placed it in the foil, added the slabs of garlic butter, and put it on the fire. The flesh was moist and salmon orange.

In hindsight, I'd like to say it tasted terrible. But it didn't. It was outstanding, maybe the best trout I've ever eaten. It's the aftertaste that continues to gnaw at my memory. Someday, I want another crack at Tasmania. I want another chance to fish with Colin, knowing now what I couldn't see then. Tasmania is a world unto itself. Its trout are sublime.

To anyone bound for Tasmania hoping to catch a glimpse of a wild Tasmanian devil, I have the following advice: don't bother. Bugs Bunny cartoons aside, you probably won't see one unless you have the misfortune to step on a devil on your way to the dunny (outhouse) in the middle of the night. You see, devils are nocturnal, meaning they're out carousing while higher life forms, like flyfishers, are dreaming of all the big ones that have gotten away. Nonetheless, be forewarned that the Tasmanian devil is a frequent topic of conversation among Tassie pub-goers banking on the culpability of foreigners to believe anything they'll say.

Of all the epithets heaped on this folkloric creature, one is certainly true: the Tasmanian devil is the ugliest mammal on earth. About three to four feet long (give or take a foot for its tail), the devil is part rat, part dog, part house cat, and part hyena. Its pink ears and snout are hairless, but the rest of its body is covered in short black fur with white markings. Cat-like whiskers sprout from its cheeks. Strictly carnivorous and extremely bad-tempered, it emerges at night from its cave or hollow log to take on anything from a small sheep to a poisonous snake. With jaws as powerful as a hyena's, the scavenging devil is also one of the few animals on earth that consumes its entire prey—fur, feathers, bones, and all.

Still, like North America's wolverine, the marsupial devil won't tangle with a person unless left with no alternative. Tangling with people, as the Tasmanian tiger discovered at the beginning of this century, can be a sure path to extinction. Most scientists believe that the last tiger, also called the Tasmanian wolf or thylacine, died in Hobart Zoo in 1936. Another marsupial, the tiger had short brown fur and looked like a wolf except for dark stripes resembling a tiger's across the rear of its back. And while the tiger barked, whined, and growled like a dog, when chased it hopped like a kangaroo on its hind legs.

But its habit of preying on sheep and poultry guaranteed its demise. European settlers in Tasmania paid large bounties for dead tigers, and by 1914 most of them had been killed off. Occasional sightings are still reported, but authorities invariably dismiss these claims as false. The only remaining tiger in Tasmania is the venomous snake of the same name.

A SNAKE IN THE GRASS

Tasmania is a good place to spot your first poisonous Australian snake. As you've no doubt gathered by now, it's also a pretty good place to catch a brown trout big enough to make you forget about snakes, but unfortunately an angler can't have one without the other.

There are three types of poisonous snakes to worry about there: the tiger, the whip, and the copperhead. I know this is true because Colin, who spends about three months a year bushwalking in the Tasmanian outback and frequently sees more snakes than fish, told me so. If you want to see a dead Australian snake, any highway will do; if you want to see a *living* snake Down Under, then Colin's your man.

My first live-snake sighting took place while standing chest-deep in Woodwards Canal, the outlet of Bronte Lagoon. It had been a slow afternoon, hot and muggy, and Colin and I were prospecting up and down the canal for the brown trout that hung their shingles there. I usually opted to fish the stillwater lagoons and lakes when I could, but when the wind came up or I just plain felt like it, the earth-bottomed canals were a great diversion. Thankfully, things never got so desperate that I had to toss a fly into one of those concrete flumes like the one draining Pine Tier Lagoon.

Woodwards Canal was lined with willows along both banks, their white blossoms contrasting with the deep green leaves, but every now and then we'd find an opening large enough to cast a fly line through.

Sometimes, where the steep drop-off eased, it was possible to wade and approach fish in the classic upstream manner. I'd found such a spot and was just about to cast to a rise tight to the near bank when something caught my eye in the water on the other side of the canal.

At first I thought it was a branch that had dropped off a tree, then I realized that this branch was quartering toward me, swimming with a serpentine motion on top of the water. Suddenly stealth seemed less important, and I slapped the water with my rod to let the snake know I wasn't a submerged stump.

The green snake, which gleamed like a Winston rod in the sunlight, altered its course and slithered up the bank into the tall grass about a dozen feet ahead of me. Just then Colin walked up from behind, ascertaining from my description that the snake was a whip. It was nice to know what it was; it would have been even nicer to know *where* it was. I still had to exit the water, after all, and how was I to know that the serpent hadn't disappeared downstream instead of up?

"Ugh, Colin . . . Would you mind going over there and thrashing around a bit?" He minded. He did, however, jump up and down where he stood in an attempt to give the snake a resounding chorus of *Good Vibrations*. We didn't see the snake again. I have no idea what the trout thought of all this, but we didn't see another rise again that afternoon, either.

A couple of days later I'd teamed up with Colin again for that bushwalk into Powena Creek and the Western Lakes. "We'll probably see a few snakes," he said. "The area is full of them." The only consolation, it seemed, was that it was just after New Year's and the Tasmanian summer had been quite cool and rainy. Colin said that that would make the snakes lethargic and discourage them from wandering too far from their holes. At the height of summer, say late January or February, he said it wasn't unusual to spot a dozen tiger snakes a day curled up on the tussocks or sunning themselves on rocks.

We'd just set up camp at Lake Fanny following the tough bushwalk in when Colin came and rustled me out of my tent. "If you want to see a tiger snake," he said, "follow me." Apparently, he'd been out looking for trout cruising along the shoreline when he'd spotted the snake sunning on a rocky outcrop. After a brief search, we found it curled up on the same rock. It looked like a dead fire hose, a little thicker and a little shorter than I'd expected. Coal black. Colin said that that was the common color phase in Tasmania. Tigers, especially on the Australian mainland, can also sport variegated stripes over the length of their bodies, hence the name.

Tip-toeing, I snuck closer in hopes of getting a picture. For some reason, the envisioned terror of my first encounter with a tiger snake didn't exist. I perceived more danger in the possibility of falling off the bluff. When Colin cautioned me and said the snake could move surprisingly fast if so inclined, I pooh-poohed the notion and raised the camera to my face. In a sweep, the snake disappeared into a hole in the rocks. It happened so quickly that I turned to Colin for confirmation, half-expecting to see it draped around his neck. My stunted view of physics said living cylinders weren't supposed to move that fast, but the Real Thing had proved me wrong. I didn't get the picture, of course, but the episode added a new dimension to my paranoia.

It wasn't until Colin and I were walking out at week's end, criss-crossing the marshy terrain on the way to Christys Creek, that I saw my second tiger snake. It was much closer than the first one; in fact, it was inches from Colin's left boot. I was walking single-file behind him when the dark flash caught my eye. He saw it at the same instant.

"Tiger!" he shouted, leaping backwards. "Tiger!"

The snake vacated the brown grassy clearing very quickly and disappeared into a clump of shrubs a few yards away. Unlike the huge inchman ant I'd see later that day, it didn't rear, and it didn't attack. It got the hell out of there as fast as it could.

You don't need to spend much time in Oz before discovering that authorities on snakes are more common than the reptiles themselves. However, the snake experts almost invariably hold second jobs like bricklaying or painting or flying commercial airplanes. Paul was no exception. He drove the mail truck, which doubled as the scheduled public bus service, between Albury and Corryong, two towns just west of the Snowies back on the Australian mainland. If you were lucky, Paul would invite you to sit up front with him and toss letters out the passenger-side window into roadside mailboxes while he swerved back and forth across the highway with practiced abandon and performed the same task on his side. Never mind that it took three hours to travel sixty miles.

Then, if you pressed him a little, Paul would tell you things about Australian snakes that, as a flyfisher, you really didn't want to know. He would tell you that nine of the world's ten deadliest land snakes live in Oz. "That other fellow must get mighty lonely," he would add.

He would tell you that black snakes bite once and let go, and that brown snakes bite and *don't* let go, pumping you full of venom while you're trying to pry a five-foot sausage with teeth off your arm, leg, or face. He would tell you that a female tiger snake will attack anyone coming between it and its young, and that any tiger snake, male or female, will attack if alarmed. Tiger snake venom, Paul would emphasize, can fell a horse in mid-stride.

If the tiger snake is starting to sound like Australia's equivalent of the grizzly bear, consider: the preferred habitat is the wet, rocky, willow-strewn ground along depressions and streambeds. This is also the preferred habitat of the flyfisher in search of brown trout. Both Paul and the Australian promotional brochures failed to mention this.

Wayne, his boss Mick, and I were fishing the Frying Pan Arm of Lake Eucumbene one night, standing side-by-side in ankle-deep water while large rainbow trout sipped invisible insects at our feet. As if having to worry about breaking an ankle in an abandoned wombat hole along the flooded lake shore wasn't enough, Wayne and Mick had to start telling me about "water rats." Be on the lookout, they said, and don't wander too far out into the water. Apparently the rats were dimwitted and spooked easily. Mick explained that in such a panicked state, they were liable to mistake an angler out in the water for a dead stump and scurry up his back to safety. It wasn't until we were driving back to Wayne's flat an hour or so later—until I'd spent the rest of the evening staring over my shoulder for something resembling a cheeky muskrat—that the pair told me they'd been pulling my leg. Nice guys.

However, Mick did have at least one true story to tell. Several years prior, he'd been wading chest-deep in a New South Wales stream when he approached the bank to rejoin his buddy.

"I reached up with my hands to pull myself up when my mate screamed," he recalled. "This big brown snake had reared up and was looking me straight in the eye. I had a metal pail in one hand and instinctively lifted it in front of my face. The snake struck and I rolled over onto the bank and started running. I reckon that critter had quite a headache, but I never stuck around to ask him."

Mick was lucky; others aren't. While hitching that ride through the Snowies with the group of river rafters, I started talking about snakes with a nurse from a Melbourne hospital. She told me about a patient of hers, an angler wearing gumboots who'd stepped over a log and startled a small brown snake. The first thing it did was seek cover, and it would have been interesting to note the look on the man's face as the snake slithered into the nearest boot.

"He was bitten twice," she recalled. "It's a miracle he lived, but he was still seeing cross-eyed two weeks later."

My first Australian snake sighting was somewhat less visceral. Driving back from that spotty brown trout fishing trip with Will on the Tumut River—where I'd seen a live dingo and a dead wombat, but no snakes—he jolted the car to a stop, threw it in reverse, and explained that he'd seen a snake on the shoulder. When the black object came into view I reluctantly leaned my head out the window, half expecting it to jump up and seize me by the nose. No such luck. It had been crushed by a tire. Expecting something on the order of the Loch Ness monster, its size startled me—two feet at best. It was black on top and red on the bottom, so it didn't surprise me when Will said it was a red-bellied black snake. Australians don't mince words when it comes to naming snakes.

Passing motorists must have wondered what I was up to, but I wasn't about to squander such a golden red-bellied opportunity. I pried its stiff jaw open with a twig and located the two small fangs at the back of its throat. They were the same diameter as small sewing needles.

"That's it?" I asked Will, who seemed disturbed by my morbid curiosity.

"Those fangs," he replied, "are big enough to kill you in a few minutes without treatment." I thought it over, and eyed the dead snake. Its forked tongue lay splayed carelessly on the asphalt. This particular snake looked anything but intimidating, but Will was right and at least now I knew what to look for.

I also knew that I was going to go blind looking for it.

The prospect of wearing gumboots during my Australian fishing exploits didn't appeal to me after that conversation with the nurse in the van, so I opted for heavy nylon chest waders instead. I felt pretty secure until an angler pointed out to me one evening that a big snake could easily sink a fang through the nylon and into my ankle. From then on, every time my ankle brushed against a shrub, I almost jumped out of my waders. At about the same time I began to notice that Australian anglers seemed to prefer the heavy, green rubber hip boots and chest waders that we North Americans generally associate with duck sloughs. Before long I spent less time looking at the water, where I should have been looking, and more time staring at the ground before my feet.

When someone asked me if I'd seen the riseform near the grass on the far bank, I was apt to respond that no, I hadn't seen the riseform, but had my partner noticed the lovely lilies growing amongst the tufts of snow grass at our feet? Fishing companions fell by the wayside. I knew I had to change my tune or come up with a better ensemble. Paranoia had sunk its fangs into my thoughts.

Picture this: you're walking along a mountainous bushwalking trail littered with bark and branches from the eucalyptus trees lining the path. Australian branches seem to fall off more than their North American counterparts, so the trail, more often than not, is completely obscured by deadfall. The branches come in various shades of brown, black, and gray—just like the snakes. Right about then your fishing companion cautions against trudging carelessly over the stick piles. "I'd keep an eye out for snakes," he says. "They like to lie-up in the sticks, and when you surprise them they're just as likely to freeze as move off." Which means, in turn, that you're just as likely to step on one as walk by it. Snakes—Australian or otherwise—don't like to be stepped on.

"Now let me get this straight," you say. "I thought the poisonous snakes here liked the wet, bushy ground along creeks and rivers."

"That's right," your companion replies.

"Okay, but now you're telling me they like lying in piles of sticks along trails."

"They like that, too," he says matter-of-factly. You weigh this for a moment and the truth is self evident: there's no safe spot to place your foot in Australia, and anglers are especially vulnerable. Suddenly the path teems with sticks. Looking for a snake amongst the sticks is like trying to find a white Kleenex on a ski hill. Your nerves condense and your eyes fall into a comatose rhythm. Focusing about a dozen feet or so ahead of you, they meticulously scan the trail foot by foot back toward you until stopping at your boot tops. Then they flick back out, and the entire process is repeated. Because you're walking, of course, the same ground is never studied twice. Think of it as prospecting along a flat stretch of water with a dry fly; reaching with the cast, retrieving . . . reaching with the cast, retrieving . . .

If this becomes tedious—which, assuredly, it will—then thank the same deity responsible for putting snakes in Australia for thoughtfully omitting bears. The thought of having to simultaneously scan for snakes at your feet and bears on the horizon is enough to make anyone see double. Who needs venom?

Later in the trip I flew from Hobart across the Tasman Sea to Christchurch to fish New Zealand's South Island. I'll talk more about the fishing there in due course, but something that happened in New Zealand is nonetheless worth mentioning now. First, I should point out that there are no snakes in New Zealand, venomous or otherwise. While there I spent a good deal of time in the Nelson Lakes area, and on one particular trip ventured alone up the Travers River above Lake Rotoiti. It had taken me several weeks, but I'd finally convinced myself that there was no reason to stare at the ground anymore. I met another flyfisher who'd recently come over from Australia, and he said he'd been trying to wean himself from the same habit. We had a good laugh about it.

On my second day up the Travers I came to a likely looking pool. The sun was still low in the sky and the glare off the water blinding. I was sight fishing now, so I crossed the river to see into the water and climbed atop a forested bluff, shaded and damp with early morning dew. Walking slowly along the edge, I carefully scrutinized the pool about forty feet below.

Suddenly I felt a sharp pain in my lower legs like I'd been stabbed by thorns or something. I looked down and my bare legs were covered in wasps, which frequented the area to suck the honey dew off the black beech trees. I'd stepped on a gopher-sized hole and the wasps were spouting out. Instinctively, I brushed at my legs and bolted for the forest to try and shake the wasps buzzing around my head. After about thirty yards I'd lost them. Stumbling to a standstill, adrenaline slowly gave way to a tingling, numbing sensation in my legs. A moment later, I watched my arms literally swell before my eyes, and an invisible grip clasped my neck and wouldn't let go. I was suffocating.

While in Oz, the guide in that van full of rafters had told me that if I was ever bitten by a poisonous snake, the best thing to do was immerse myself in cold water and lie motionless. Something about lowering the blood pressure and slowing down the metabolism and, thus, the spread of venom. Since I was suffocating anyway, it seemed worth a try. The nearest help was at least two or three hours down-stream. I struggled to the water and lay in the river up to my neck. The cool flow enveloped my body and a narrowing window of sky enveloped my mind. I thought I was going to die.

Then, slowly, the pressure eased. I sat up and studied the multitude of bites on my legs, which seemed detached and remote in the shim-mering current, suspended in the water like blanched salmon. It took me three hours to walk back down the river to the alpine hut where I was staying at the edge of the lake. There was no one else there and walk-ing out was impossible given my condition, so I spent the afternoon bundled in a down sleeping bag, alternating between hot and cold, sleeping and wakefulness. That night I vomited so hard and frequently that I finally tired of lighting and extinguishing the candle, and lay down with a head-lamp strapped through my sweaty hair instead.

The next morning I heard a boat and was salvaged by a family hol-idaying at the lake-side town of St. Arnaud. I spent almost a week con-valescing, and a doctor said that lying in the water during the allergic reaction had probably saved my life. There are no snakes in New

Zealand, but I feel indebted to that whitewater rafting guide in Australia for his snake bite advice.

I carry an adrenaline syringe now whenever I'm fishing in case I'm bitten by a wasp or a bee. Nevertheless, old habits die hard. I still study the ground before my feet a lot, snakes or not, but I figure a man can do worse than watch his step.

As if good flyfishing gear isn't expensive enough in North America, Down Under it can break your personal bank. And don't be deceived by the stronger American or Canadian dollars, either. Whether it be rods, reels, fly tying materials, or any of the other angling paraphernalia flyfishers hoard like squirrels, you could wind up plunking some serious cash on the fly shop counters down there, so be forewarned.

Wayne gave me a brief run-down on the state of Aussie fly tying one afternoon while we were fooling around at his bench. Good materials, it seemed, were either really expensive or impossible to get. Even if you could find one in the shops—which you couldn't—he said a #1 Metz cape was about $75 (American). It goes without saying that most fly tiers there resigned themselves to using lousy hackle. Even some of the guides I met used imported flies, and that probably says more than anything else.

Wayne and Murray didn't face the same fiscal hardships when it came to rods, because Murray had managed to import Loomis rods wholesale from the U.S. through his shop. In fact, he'd offered to order me a four-piece IMX six-weight and sell it to me wholesale, but it still would have cost about $350. (The retail price was about $500!) As it was, it would have taken too long to get there, so I passed.

The Aussies and especially the New Zealanders manufactured several of their own brands of graphite rods, but quality-wise, what would be considered a mid-priced rod in the U.S. still fetched between $200 and $300 in either country. When it came time for me to buy a six-weight rod in Christchurch, built in-shop from Sage graphite III blanks, it cost $450. Needless to say, whether I use it or not, I've still convinced myself that it's my favorite rod.

A top-quality fly line in New Zealand would set you back over $50, and in Oz, one of the popular American flyfishing magazines (an Australian publisher came out with the first edition of a flyfishing-only magazine just before I arrived) was about $7. The moral here, if there is one, is to cart everything you'll possibly need in the way of fishing gear over with you on the plane. It's not my intention to knock the Down Under retailers, but when it comes to doing business, the costs of importing fishing tackle from North America and Europe can't help but inflate prices.

THE FROG KILLER AND MRS. SIMPSON

I am thinking of an item torn from a Calgary newspaper. It's a small item, a single column, and I have it stuck to the fridge with a magnet. It's called the "Angling Tips Line," and it lists a number of local rivers and lakes and instructs anglers on how to go about catching fish in them. It says that the fishing has been good in such-and-such a river: "Use smaller patterns of dry flies." It says that the fishing has been so-so in such-and-such a lake: "The walleye are biting jigs and leeches first thing in the morning."

And then it says this. "**South Saskatchewan River:** People are catching sturgeon in selected spots along the river. Try using Cornish game hens or chicken guts. Remember, sturgeon under three feet long must be thrown back."

I put this on the fridge because it got me to thinking: has anyone ever fished for sturgeon with a fly rod? Is is possible to cast a Cornish game hen with an eight-weight? Could a fly of natural materials be tied to imitate chicken guts? The possibilities—not to mention the questions—are endless. Still, I didn't get around to flyfishing for sturgeon this summer. Maybe next year.

The newspaper item also got me to thinking about natural bugs and what lengths flyfishers will go to to imitate them. Sometimes the imitations are quite good. A no-hackle, split-tail, quill-wing mayfly dun *does* look an awful lot like the insect perched on the brim of your hat. Other times, of course, the imitations aren't so hot, but the fish seem to like them anyway. Borger's Fleeing Crayfish looks more like a gaudy Christmas tree ornament than a crustaccan; LaFontaine's Halo Mayfly Emerger bears more resemblance to a lilliputian extraterrestrial than an emerging dun. And then, lurking in the tepid trout streams of eastern Australia, there is the Frog Killer.

The Frog Killer is a fly. That's not to say, of course, that Australian flies kill frogs; rather, the Frog Killer is a fly tied to *imitate* a frog. As demonstrated by Wayne and Murray, it also does a pretty good job of catching Australian trout.

Wayne handed me my first Frog Killer one evening on a grassy bank beside the Moonbah River. The light was fading quickly and the air had that heavy, humid feel to it that presses down on your shoulders and threatens to douse your head in the creek. The fly was medium sized, tied on a size 8 hook, and basically consisted of two green-dyed guinea fowl feathers with black polka dots tied side-by-side against the shank.

It didn't look much like a frog. Of course, as Wayne patiently explained, it was so dark by then that it really didn't matter if it looked much like a frog. The idea was to fish it close to the surface, casting slightly upstream and then stripping the line back in short, quick jerks in an attempt to make like a frog swimming from one bank to the other.

I've got buddies back home who use the same technique with a Woolly Bugger to deceive nocturnal brown trout. The general theory is that it doesn't matter how dark it is, because the trout senses the disturbance in the water the same way a shark senses a thrashing swimmer. The outcome is often the same as well—a violent take. Personally, I've always found fishing like that a bit unnerving. My concerns aren't so much with the trout as with things that go bump in the night. Good Lord, deliver me!

On my third cast or so with the Frog Killer the line stopped in midstream and the darkness echoed with the sound a beaver makes when it slaps its tail on the surface of the water. The line slithered from between my thumb and index finger, and instinctively I knew I was into a good fish. Wayne knew it, too, and watched as the trout sounded and wrapped the leader around a submerged clump of weeds. The rod sprang straight, and Wayne had his fly box out and a new Frog Killer in his hand before I could reel in.

"Try it again," he said. I switched my headlamp on and struggled to feed the severed line through the hook's eye in the narrow beam of light. No sooner was the fly back in the water than we heard another splash. This time I managed to land the fish, a small brown, and we admired it beneath the headlamp before slipping it back into the stream and watching it vanish from our limited field of vision.

I hooked several more trout that way in short order and began thinking, in a roundabout sort of way, of the thousands of *real* frogs which must have perished each summer without ever glimpsing that far side of the stream. *Why did the frog cross the river?* For the same reason the chicken crossed the road, I guess.

The bats must have known why the frogs crossed the river because one tried to hitch a ride in the opposite direction when it plucked the Frog Killer out of mid-air during a backcast. The line's forward momentum carried the bat as far as midstream before dumping it unceremoniously in the water. At first I thought I'd snagged a clump of grass or a small tree branch but discovered the bat when I reeled in and found it soaked and rumpled with the fly dangling embarrassingly from the corner of its furry mouth. Wayne cradled it in his baseball cap while I performed the necessary surgery. It flew away unharmed.

Suddenly the Frog Killer had assumed Edwardian proportions: here was a pattern that seemingly did it all. By sea, by land, by air . . . the U.S. Marines had nothing on the Frog Killer.

One of the most interesting things about flyfishing Down Under is comparing the natural insects to those in North America. Bugs being bugs, there really isn't much difference, say, between a caddisfly in Oz and a caddisfly in Canada. The color and size may vary—I saw caddisflies in Australia so white they glowed in the dark—but, let's face it, they vary a lot from state to state and river to river, too. Of even greater interest, at least as far as I am concerned, is comparing the patterns flyrodders have come up with to imitate the same bug on opposite sides of the world.

The grasshopper is a good example. During the long, hot, dry summers so common to eastern Australia, grasshoppers can represent the only chance an angler has of catching trout on a dry fly for weeks, if not months, on end. Predictably, Australian fly tiers hold hoppers in great esteem.

It might be a crass generalization, but Down Under hopper patterns have evolved quite differently than their North American counterparts. For instance, with the exception of a few transplanted Americans trying to pass themselves off as Aussies, the fly tiers I met there were still reluctant to incorporate deer hair into their hoppers, something North American fly tiers almost take for granted.

I talked about this with Wayne one night; his theory was that it's really tough to find quality deer hair in many of the Australian shops. Fair enough. Instead, most of the Aussie hopper patterns are heavily hackled with a brightly colored downwing—often golden pheasant tippet—and a yellow chenille body: the Glen Innes Hopper, O'Briens Hopper, and the Snowy Mountain Hopper all fit the bill. There is the odd exception. For example, the Muddler Hopper (also called the Nobby Hopper) is basically a variation of the dry-style North American Muddler Minnow and seemed to be catching on.

At one time or another I tried using most of these patterns and, setting prejudice aside, still prefer a deer hair hopper for its buoyancy and visibility. Each to their own, however, because I saw Aussies catch plenty of trout on grasshoppers *sans* the deer hair.

Strangely enough, the Aussies and New Zealanders have been far less reluctant to incorporate deer and elk hair into their caddisfly imitations. Troth's Elk Hair Caddis and Goddard's Caddis in sizes 10 through 16 seemed to be the patterns of choice in both countries to imitate the sporadic Down Under caddis hatches.

Mayflies are a different story. In fact, compared to the heavy mayfly hatches so common to North American rivers, the order Ephemeroptera is something of an enigma Down Under. In short, you just won't find the weekly, daily, and even hourly mayfly hatches there that you will on rivers like Montana's Missouri or Alberta's Bow. That's not to say it doesn't happen—I stumbled across some damn good mayfly fishing on occasion in Tasmania and on New Zealand's South Island—but rather, that it doesn't happen as often.

Sometimes, especially if you've been raised on the sort of mayfly fishing where you'll get two or three great hatches of different species in the course of a single day, this gets downright frustrating. I spent almost a week in New Zealand along the banks of the placid and relatively obscure Taieri River. Each afternoon and evening were the same as the last—clear, calm, and not a fish showing anywhere. This last observation can probably be attributed to the fact that there wasn't an insect showing anywhere, either.

I'd sit on a stump along the bank, nibbling on a strand of grass while I stared blankly at the glassy water and contemplated another non-event. The water temperature seemed right and local farmers kept talking about the Taieri's great evening rises, but the only things rising each day were *my* temperature and the resolve to return twenty-four hours later. It's easy for a flyfisher to get caught up in a vicious cycle at a time like that. You know that sooner or later that great evening rise is going to materialize, and one of Murphy's flyfishing laws clearly states that it's going to materialize the evening *after* you clear out of the county, screaming defeat.

"Well, mate," the fellow on a bar stool in the next county will tell you several days later, "I hear the Taieri's fishing *real* well. Evening rises so thick they'll lift the hat from your head and carry it off."

So you hang in there, afraid to leave, compelled to stay. I've seen it happen to duck hunters, gamblers—even the guy who mistakenly shows up a day early for the big football game. I stayed beside the Taieri until I was sick from eating grass and that stump had worn a hole in my butt. And then, without looking back, I stood up and left. I didn't want to look back because I feared that if I did, I might have seen a mayfly, and that, quite frankly, would have ticked me off forever.

If there's a general rule of thumb regarding Down Under mayfly patterns, it's that natural materials still rule and the British influence is still paramount. You won't find anything like a Comparadun at all there, but every shop has a large selection of flies like Greenwell's Glory, Twilight Beauty, and Hardy's Favourite. While North American fly tiers are forging ahead with synthetic materials and innovative designs, Down Under flyfishers appear content with the old standbys. And why not? They work, after all, and sometimes I think that we North Americans go a little overboard in our zeal to create new patterns for natural insects that have been around for thousands, if not millions, of years. Face it, the intelligence flyfishers anthropomorphically bestow on trout is absurd. I was fortunate enough to learn to fly-fish under the tutelage of Bow River guide Brian Anderson, who never let fiction get in the way of fact.

"If it's the right size and the right shape, the trout will take it," he repeated *ad nauseam*. "Flyfishermen that think otherwise can usually stand to work on their casting."

Brian's theory is that presentation is everything. It's a pretty good theory in North America; by the time I arrived at the mountainous freestone streams of New Zealand, I realized that it's a pretty good theory there, too. The reality there is that many a day passes when you won't see a single bug on the water. No insects, no hatches. Amazingly, the huge rainbow and brown trout there still occasionally rise to a well-presented dry fly. I have no idea why, but it happens and watching it happen, especially when the dry fly is attached to your fly line, is thrill enough for anyone.

It should come as no surprise then that under such circumstances an attractor pattern is the fly of choice. New Zealanders are inordinately fond of Royal Wulffs, Green Humpies, and Yellow Humpies in sizes 10 through 16, but I had better success with a size 14 Irresistible. The trout seemed less inclined to refuse it than a white-winged pattern: one theory is that they see so many Wulffs tossed by heli-anglers during the course of a season that a fish automatically associates the fly with an angler at the other end of the line.

But alas, Brian would be appalled, because I've fallen into the trap of giving the trout more credit than they deserve. Even when the fish were feeding on beetles (supposedly one of flyfishing's greatest challenges) I took nice trout on any of a half-dozen popular patterns, including the Red Tag, Coch-y-bondu, and Gum Beetle. Just like Brian says, size, shape, and a good cast generally got the job done.

The New Zealand and Australian trout are equally unselective in their choice of nymphs. In fact, before long I began to refer to "that blue nymph" or "this brown nymph," and the only time I'd ever catch the names was when I bought the next dozen or so at a fly shop. The Hare & Copper (similar to a North American Hare's Ear) and

Pheasant Tail in sizes 12 through 16 were by far the most productive for me, but nymphs like the March Brown, Woolly Worm, and Seals Fur in brown, black, and green accounted for a few fish as well.

Another good Aussie pattern, particularly when the rainbows are intercepting shore-bound dragonfly nymphs in the large Australian lakes such as Jindabyne and Eucumbene, is the Mudeye. When I first arrived in Oz I overheard a couple of anglers in a shop talking about Mudeye this and Mudeye that: I just assumed it was the Aussie way of referring to a vicious mud-slinging contest at water's edge. Not so. The Mudeye, it turned out, is one of the deadliest patterns in Oz, especially when fished from lake shores with quick, short strips. An odd-looking pattern, the Mudeye has a compact chenille body, feather downwing, and bulbous bead eyes that only recently have come into vogue in North America.

Yet another strange Aussie stillwater pattern is the Yabby, patterned after the giant freshwater crayfish of the same name. I glimpsed my first living yabby along the shore of Lake Jindabyne while fishing with Wayne and Murray. With its oversized claws and probing antennae, your first inclination may be to pick up a yabby, throw it into a pot of boiling water, and start melting butter. Indeed, to someone used to see-ing shrimp along the lines of a size 12 Bighorn scud, your average yabby looks like it could hold its own against Godzilla in the streets of down-town Tokyo. "It won't hurt you," Wayne assured me. The yabby in question was pinkish orange, and, if it was possible to say such a thing about a primitive crustacean with pencil-point eyes, it leered at me intently. To tell you the truth, it sort of gave me the creeps.

So did the eels. A discussion of Down Under flies wouldn't be complete without talking about eels. I know, I know . . . what the hell do eels and flies have to do with one another? Well, the connection between eels and flies, at least as far as I could tell, was that the former absolutely, unfailingly refuses to eat the latter. I never saw an eel eat a fly. It wasn't for lack of trying to get one to either.

The first time I seriously cast to an eel was on New Zealand's Twizel River. I was walking along a gravel bar looking for fish, but the only thing showing in the pool was this damn eel rummaging around along the far bank about thirty feet away. Eels don't swim, they rummage. Actually, they sort of glide curiously along a bank, pausing under a rock, slipping beneath an undercut, sliding behind a stump. They move the same way a kid moves on his way to the cookie jar, the same way a cat moves on its way past the doghouse.

This particular eel seemed to be enjoying itself. A little *too* much, I decided, so I tied on a large Woolly Bugger and lobbed it across the river. The eel ignored it. I tied on a small nymph and lobbed it across the river. The eel ignored that, too. The truth is, the eel ignored me and my flies altogether.

Eels may not like flies, but unlike me, they love things that go bump in the night. Mice. Frogs. A big toe. I met a hiker once who swore an eel had latched on to his big toe. He was a lot bigger than me, so I nodded and said sure, why not, a big toe. Stranger things have happened. There are stories told of New Zealand deer cullers in the days of old who set out to cross waist-deep rivers with bloody carcasses draped across their shoulders. Like those frogs back on the Moonbah, they never made it to the far bank. Legend has it that eels the size of sewer pipes smelled the blood dripping into the water, swarmed the poor victim, and dragged him under.

There are stories told of scuba divers who ventured into the murky depths of New Zealand's largest lakes, saw eels big enough to bite their arms off, and barely made it back to the surface, gasping and scared witless. Anglers also have their share of eel stories, some true, some not. The one I heard most often and had no reason to doubt is that eels sometimes smelled a bleeding fish and came to investigate. This never happened to me, but I once had a New Zealander who fished with bait tell me about a nice rainbow he'd hooked being attacked by eels and torn apart piece by piece before his disbelieving eyes. There are places in New Zealand where you can watch the locals toss scraps of meat to frenzied eels, and after I witnessed such a spectacle, the man's story didn't seem farfetched at all.

And yet, as I've said, I never saw an eel take a fly. I saw them caught on hand lines and taken out of traps, but every time I cast a fly at one I got the same indifferent response. Even the Edwardian Frog Killer failed to entice the eels. Even Mrs. Simpson.

Mrs. Simpson is a fly. She looks a lot like the Frog Killer except that the two feathers tied side-by-side along the shank, an overskirt of sorts, are pheasant and not guinea fowl. Her petticoat is red chenille, her scarf black thread, and like the Frog Killer, she's best fished at night by stripping the line back in short, quick jerks. At least that's the theory. I never actually hooked a fish on a Mrs. Simpson, although I did see Wayne hook one.

He took a healthy sixteen-inch rainbow out of Lake Eucumbene one night when all else was failing. We'd tried emergers, tiny midges, nymphs—nothing worked. Then, frustrated beyond logic, Wayne tied on a Mrs. Simpson and lofted her into the nearest riseform. The fly hadn't been in the water two seconds when the dark surface was jolted by an electric take and Wayne hollered that he had a fish on. While he played the trout farther down the shoreline, I reached inside my vest pocket and pulled out the streamer box. I turned on my headlamp and started to tie a Mrs. Simpson to the tippet, but she was too much to handle and I dropped her in the lake. She sank to the bottom, disappeared, and there were no more Mrs. Simpsons where she came from.

She lies there to this day, I suppose, on the bottom of the lake. Poor Mrs. Simpson: all dressed up and no place to go.

New Zealanders are commonly referred to as Kiwis, both by themselves and others. The kiwi is a flightless bird, grayish brown, and looks a bit like a chicken-sized quail with Larry Bird's legs and Pinocchio's nose. Both nocturnal and extremely shy, kiwis use their long, yellowish bills with nostrils on the end to sniff out worms and small insects. But while New Zealanders talk about them affectionately, Aussies are liable to point out that kiwis are lazy, good-for-nothing birds that sleep as much as twenty hours a day. That pretty much sums up how Aussies feel about New Zealanders, too. The longer I spent Down Under, the more obvious it became that Aussies and Kiwis really don't like each other very much. Often they'll try to brush this off as good-natured rivalry, but I wasn't buying any of it.

No sooner did I step off the plane in Christchurch than I got to see things from the Kiwi point of view. The customs agent there solemnly asked to see the fishing gear that I'd just carted over from Tasmania. The four-piece fly rod was no problem. Ditto for the flies, which because they were tied from natural feathers and hair, I'd half-expected to be confiscated under the Kiwi agricultural quarantine.

No, the things that were causing all the problems were the neoprene feet on my chest waders, which were flecked with dried mud, and the tattered mesh fabric on the outside of my wading boots, which was sprouting grass and seeds.

"You'll have to wash that off," the agent said, explaining that New Zealand's pristine waters could ill-afford to be contaminated by a noxious Australian kernel or two. Leading me into a back room (I'm sure the people in the lineup had their own theories about the grass I was transporting), the agent took me to a large metal sink, handed me a wire scrub brush, and said he'd be back in a few minutes to see how I was coming along. Satisfied with the job I'd done, he led me to my waiting backpack. All the other tourists had long since cleared out. The agent, no longer on public display, wiped the solemn look off his face with a grin.

"I do a bit of flyfishing myself," he said proudly. "So tell me, how's the fishing over in Oz?" We started talking and before you know it, the agent had slipped a piece of paper into my hand with the names of four or five rivers. So much for first impressions.

NEW ZEALAND

TASMAN
SEA

PACIFIC
OCEAN

NORTH ISLAND

Auckland

Lake
Taupo

Taupo

Mohaka
River

Gisborne

New Plymouth

Ngaruroro
River

Mangaweka

Rangitikei
River

Nelson

Wellington

Lake
Rotoroa

St. Arnaud

Murchison

Lake
Rotoiti

Travers
River

Ikamatua

SOUTH ISLAND

Arthur's Pass

Christchurch

Twizel

Worsley
Stream

Queenstown

Waipiata

Lake
Te Anau

Te Anau

Mararoa
River

Mossburn

Oreti
River

Dunedin

Invercargill

STEWART
ISLAND

The route of the author's
journey through New Zealand
by bus, car, plane, boat and foot.

Map by Fiona Kirkpatrick

PART II – NEW ZEALAND

WHEN THE WIND IS IN THE EAST

My first New Zealand flyfishing lesson took place in a Christchurch backyard. There was a two-car garage on one side, a willow tree on the other, and about thirty feet of optic orange fly line laid out on the grass in between.

Bob Vaile, a transplanted Canadian from Calgary and former Bow River guide, crouched over the last dozen feet or so and dabbed at the line with a black felt pen. The line quickly absorbed the sticky ink in the midday sun, and black and orange combined to produce a pleasing shade of chocolate brown.

"There," Bob said, hoisting his muscled, ursine body off the ground. Tanned with dark, straight hair, he had a neatly trimmed goatee and a gold stud in one ear that flashed in the sun. "You might get away with orange line back home, but here it spooks fish." Now, I know what you're thinking. *Bull!* Right? Whether it be in New Zealand, North America, or anywhere else in the world, for that matter, the line-color debate prompts more arguments than a family dinner. But the bottom line was that Bob was doing me a favor and I was his guest. When in New Zealand, I figured, do as Kiwis do and keep your mouth shut.

Anyway, Bob then nail-knotted a seventeen-foot leader to the end of my new indelible line. At the time, I didn't have the heart to tell him that I could still recall a day when seventeen feet constituted a passable *cast* for me.

It didn't matter. Two hours later I was casting over my first New Zealand spring creek, Bob was on the far bank and what had discreetly been left unsaid was now painfully obvious to him, myself, and the two or three frightened brown trout I'd already spooked along the way. Yet another now swung lazily from side to side about twenty-five feet upstream of where I knelt among a showy tuft of grass. A discernible seam split the peat-stained current where it rounded a small willow clinging to the bank. The trout, poised in the slack water near the shore, would periodically sway to the right to intercept an underwater tidbit.

The pendulum act continued unabated while my nervous fingers knotted themselves trying to tie a nondescript, weighted "brown nymph" to a 3x tippet. The northwest wind, sweeping down from the Southern Alps with enough force to flip the brim of my cap up against my forehead, only made matters worse. I'd never wanted to catch a fish so badly.

"The wind's gusting," Bob shouted. "Let out enough line in the water behind you, and when the wind dies down put the schtick to the rod and turn it over. You shouldn't have to falsecast at all."

I tried, but just when it seemed the wind was dropping off, it picked up again and I bailed out mid-cast. The slack line caught in the breeze and wound up making a pretty fair presentation to the far bank. Which, you'll recall, is where Bob was sitting.

"What," he asked disgustedly, "was that?" Now at that point, I wasn't as worried about impressing Bob as catching my first New Zealand trout. I let the comment pass and tried another cast. Twenty minutes later I'd described a neat arc around the fish with my flies, but as Bob pointed out, I still hadn't hit the *spot* yet. If it was this discouraging after less than twenty-four hours in New Zealand, I asked myself, then what was it going to be like three weeks from now?

"Go!" Bob yelled, and my reverie was shattered by the realization that I had no idea what he was talking about. I'd lost the beige wool indicator in the sun's glare and continued stripping line absurdly. "GO!" he screamed louder.

If he'd shouted "Set the hook!" maybe I'd have figured it out. But I didn't. Unbeknownst to me, the trout was swimming downstream with my nymph in its mouth, and Bob was yelling at me to do something about it. The fish figured it out, though, and darted for cover the moment it swam down far enough to see the stunned look on my face.

Bob glared at me from across the stream, his imposing bulk impressive in the tall grass, and I wasn't sure what would happen next. I was ready for anything. Then a strange thing took place. Bob dropped to the ground and started laughing, rolling around like he'd been felled by a seizure. "Brian sent you to me . . . Brian sent you to me . . . " he kept repeating, and I could only assume he meant Bow River guide Brian Anderson, a mutual friend and the one who'd slipped Bob's phone number into my pocket.

I started laughing, too, ready for a padded cell, and we kept on laughing until Bob jumped up and wandered away. It was the second important flyfishing lesson of the day. I decided at that moment to like Bob Vaile, because try as I might, disliking him was out of the question.

My meeting Bob was inevitable. While planning my trip Down Under, everyone kept talking about this crazy Calgarian that I *had* to contact in New Zealand. Bow River guru Jim McLennan mentioned him and so did old university friends. Seemed he led a John Gierach-sort of life; working when the mood struck, earning just enough money to fish, and that was it.

The truth didn't disappoint. I called Bob within hours of that encounter with the customs agent at the Christchurch airport, and Bob told me to stay put and he'd come by the downtown hostel to pick me up. "Look for a red Land Rover," he said. To be honest, all I expected was a little good advice and maybe a map or two. No sooner did Bob whisk me into his suburban bungalow than I discovered he'd sold it. Planning to store his possessions at a friend's place in the country, he'd quit his job several months earlier and intended to fish and hunt himself into oblivion.

The first thing he did was usher me into his den, pop a video in the recorder, and make me watch mouth-watering footage of him and his Kiwi buddies landing ten-pound-plus brown trout on remote South Island rivers. A midway carney couldn't have come up with a better sales pitch. Bob made it clear right away that he didn't fish stillwater, but that if I wanted, he had a couple of days to spare and maybe we could check out a few of the nearby streams and rivers. I wanted.

After both failing to hook a trout and discovering Bob's propensity for streamside theatrics on our first outing, we joined forces with Kiwi Steve Smith, loaded up the Land Rover, and bounced our way westward into the North Canterbury district and several of Bob's favorite freestone rivers. The rolling foothills could have been in Alberta, the major difference being that the sheep outnumbered the cows and not vice versa. New Zealand is as noted for its sheep as Oz is for its kangaroos. The sheep number up to 100 million during lambing season—thirty sheep for every New Zealander. Needless to say, lamb and mutton are never in short supply at the butcher's.

There were other reminders that this wasn't the countryside of home. Driving along, Bob pointed out a solitary tree in a field that he called a cabbage tree but looked to me like a miniature palm. Common throughout the plains and foothills, in times past its knife-like leaves were used by the native Maoris for rope, thatching, and medicine. Bob, ever the gracious host, soon decided that it was time to peruse some scenery of a different sort.

"Well, mate," he said to Steve less than half an hour into the journey. "I think it's about that time. Don't you?" That was my introduction to New Zealand meat pies and Ward's Canterbury draft. The pies came in one size and various combinations of beef, chicken, and pork. The draft came in lots of sizes (Kiwis are as fond of suds as the Aussies), but somehow we always seemed to settle for the jugs. "No use taking up more of the bartender's time than we need to," Bob would say, and Steve nodded in agreement, his boyish good looks and tousled hair reminding me of the cartoon character Calvin of *Calvin and Hobbes*.

Sometimes, especially if it was raining outside and the fishing was off and it was three o'clock in the morning, Steve would *begin* to nod in agreement but not quite finish the task. His head would sort of flounder at the halfway point between yes and no, dangling resignedly like a trout waiting for you to either take the hook out of its mouth or bonk it on the head.

It was during one of these lulls between a pint and a pie that I managed to learn a bit more about Bob and what had sent him packing to

New Zealand in the first place. A fishing trip in the mid-eighties had whetted his appetite to the point where he knew he had to return. When the opportunity arose in 1988 to make the return a permanent one, Bob rose at the chance and departed Canada in a flashy swirl. Sponsored by a prominent Christchurch firm, officially he emigrated as a Chartered Accountant. Friends and family knew better.

For the first few years Bob basically had to relearn how to fish. North American freshwater tactics are marginally effective in New Zealand; for instance, on some of the rivers we fished you wouldn't see a rise all day. Because the mountainous headwaters hold big fish but not a lot of them, blind prospecting with either nymph or dry fly isn't really an alternative. The trick is to learn to spot the fish before they spot you; stalking the bank with heron-like stealth, working into position, and casting upstream with a weighted nymph on a long leader.

Now don't get me wrong. A dry fly still tempts trout on occasion, but embellished fish tales aside, this is primarily an underwater game. Even then, as Bob and Steve soon demonstrated, fly size and color are not as important as an accurate drift with a minimum of false casting. In other words, it's generally a one-shot affair, and a hunting analogy isn't farfetched.

Bob had his own theories about fly selection. He'd tie on any nymph to start with, agreeing with Brian that presentation is the key. If the fish ignored the fly or swung at it but refused to take, he'd immediately switch flies and color. He generally started big, with, say, a size 8, then went smaller and smaller until the fish either took the fly or spooked. I watched him catch a lot of trout this way, so I can vouch that it worked. Well-known American flyfishing authority Jack Dennis reportedly used a nifty variation of the same principle to catch fish in New Zealand: he'd tie five or six different nymphs to the same leader, open his casting loop, and drift the entire smorgasbord past the sighted trout. I'm not sure if a fish is capable of having an orgasm, but this is a sure way to find out.

It took Bob several years to feel his way around the land and landowners, but his knowledge is now such that Kiwi guides call him for information. He still walks by a lot of fish, but he *doesn't* walk by a lot of fish, too, and I guess that's the point.

The next morning Bob, Steve, and I were standing at the tail of a large aquamarine pool. All I'm allowed to say about the river is that it's uniformly rocky, winding back and forth along a huge glacial flood-plain, and that it's situated somewhere between Christchurch and the Tasman Sea. A violent southwest wind was blowing, but that was nothing new. It was blowing downstream as usual, straight into our faces. As Bob oft repeated, "You learn to cast flies into the wind in New Zealand, or you don't cast flies at all."

Defeated, I wasn't casting flies. Bob and Steve were. Neatly spaced throughout the fifty-yard pool were about five or six brown trout—the largest trout I'd ever seen in moving water. Every now and then they entered into a territorial dispute, and a larger one chased a smaller one off its turf like a pit bull chasing a rottweiler across the street. The black shadows wavered in the current, and Bob kept telling me to calm down while he crouched behind Steve and directed his casts. I had a cancerous lump in my throat and I wasn't even holding a fishing rod. Then it happened. Steve worked out enough line to drive a size 8 bluish nymph about a dozen feet over the nearest shadow.

"Watch that one," Bob intoned, and I knew that while he and Steve had trained themselves to stare fixedly at the wool indicator tied by a slip knot to the leader, my eyes danced an anxious jig between the wool and the surging fish beneath it. The great white gob opened, the fabric was there and then it wasn't, and I was staring at Steve's seven-weight Winston and wondering how anything could bend so much without breaking. Ten minutes later Bob hefted the silvery brown into the net and glanced at the scale built into the handle. "Six-and-a-half pounds," he told Steve. "Good job, Smithy."

I needed a reference point. "How many inches?" I asked. Bob and Steve stared at me like I'd asked them to describe the life cycle of a manuka beetle.

"We don't measure fish in inches," Bob explained. I guess it would have been too much like buying milk by the fluid ounce.

That evening at the backcountry hut Bob and Steve were toasting the day's successes while I wondered if I was ever going to catch a trout in New Zealand. The one-room, wood-and-tin hut was a facsimile of the hundreds of other alpine huts dotting the New Zealand landscape. Many are operated by the federal Department of Conservation and available to the public for between $2 and $7 per night on a first-come, first-served basis. Others are on private stations (large farms or ranches) and off-limits to trampers, the Kiwi term for bushwalkers or backpackers. Either way, the huts range from crude shelters for sitting out storms (category four) to lavish buildings with cooking facilities, mattresses, toilets, and running water (category one).

Many of the huts are throwbacks to the days of New Zealand's professional deer cullers, a time not too long ago when the government actually employed people to go out and shoot a daily quota. The introduction of red deer to New Zealand in 1881 seemed like a good idea to English settlers out for a little sport. Other deer species followed, as did wild goats, Austrian chamois, Himalayan tahr, and even the North American moose, which although now believed to be extinct, nonetheless has a Sasquatch-like tendency to be spotted every now and then. But despite the Englishmen's good intentions, the game, both literally and figuratively, soon got out of hand.

Lacking natural predation (the only indigenous New Zealand mammals were bats) and blessed with an abundance of lush forage, the ungulate population soared to the point where the native flora and fauna were being seriously depleted. Enter the deer cullers, many of whom stayed in the huts for months on end, killing thousands of deer annually. The deer population was finally checked a couple of decades ago when helicopters came into vogue and cullers could simply hover above a herd and open fire. Yet, the Englishmen's meddling ways had already caused irreparable damage. For instance, when rabbits introduced as a food source in 1838 became pestilent, stoats and weasels were introduced in 1885 to try and control them. However, all that accomplished was to decimate native flightless birds like the kakapo, takahe, and the kiwi. Simply put, in many ways New Zealand resembles a mad zoology experiment run amok.

Bob and Steve, of course, fit right in. "We have a surprise for you," Bob announced at the hut that night. Reaching into their packs, he and Steve yanked out two of the most ridiculous hats I'd ever seen.

They looked like a cross between a Nepalese sherpa's hat and a clump of seaweed: dyed wool with Day-Glo trim, long spindly tassels, earflaps—the whole bit.

"Hut hats," Bob said, a grin splitting his face. See things my way for a moment. I'd already tried to overlook the fact that Bob had a gold stud in his ear. The goatee? Well, it went with his personality. But the hut hats were too much. The final straw. "Those are the ugliest hats in the world," I said, and he and Steve beamed like I'd just handed them an Oscar at the Academy Awards. It was time for an acceptance speech. They slipped on olive knee-length wool cardigans, standing there like escapees from King Arthur's court. "*Omm pa . . . Omm pa . . .*" they chanted, the beginning of the hut mantra. "*Argh . . . Argh . . . Argh . . .*"

Bob and Steve had to leave the next day to tie up some loose ends in the city, but Bob arranged to meet me on another river a day's hike and one mountain range away. It was an easy tramp by Rocky Mountain standards, the well-used trail winding through silent beech forests on the eastern flank of the Southern Alps. The only hazard worth worrying about was the odd alpine spaniard, an unusual flower that sends a single appendage armed with half-foot thorns several feet into the air. Many an angler has inadvertently straddled one of these things while studying the water: few have been aroused. Bob had his own name for the spaniard—"Satan's penis."

I spent the night alone in another hut, and just after breakfast I spotted the familiar red Land Rover coming across the field. The weather was perfect—no wind. For the first time since my arrival in New Zealand, I felt like I had a chance.

We'd been on the river less than five minutes when we spotted the first fish. The sun was already high and, with our Polaroids on, it stood out like a damaged thumb. I made a decent cast to the head of the pool, watched the indicator dart beneath the surface, and set the hook. The weight at the end of the line was bullish, but the bull charged and the hook came free. My luck was holding.

About two hundred yards upstream Bob was scouting the slack water along the near bank when I glanced across and saw a large mouth break the surface in midstream. I grabbed Bob's elbow, directed his gaze and sure enough, the trout rose to ingest another bug. We weren't sure what it was taking; the only insects in evidence were the size 28 sandflies trying to siphon the blood from our arms. Sandflies are a noxious New Zealand insect that can, particularly along the West Coast, put "mozzies" to shame. Inflicting a painful bite that festers for days if you scratch the itch, sandflies are worse along running water and on overcast days. If it's any consolation, as Bob was quick to point out, "They're slow to set up."

So was the big trout. Actually, the fish wasn't so much rising as lying on the surface with its mouth open. Bob said he'd never seen anything like it. I know I hadn't; the closest thing being the scene in *Jaws* where the shark climbs up on the end of the boat and waits for the captain to come to papa. Bob hooked and lost the fish on a size 12 Irresistible, muttered something about the trout being *too* hungry, and moved on.

Then, as if by design, I finally met the fish dumb enough to be my match. While Bob watched from an elevated clearing on the treed far bank, I snuck up behind a boulder and simply flicked a size 10 Hare & Copper (a Kiwi cross between a Hare's Ear and a Pheasant Tail) in the path of a feeding fish. When that five-and-a-half-pound brown saw that fuzzy nymph come drifting past, it almost cartwheeled in a frenzied attempt to chase it downstream. Even with feet of slack, I managed to set the hook. The trout was average by New Zealand standards, but Bob was much too circumspect to mention it. "Sometimes," he quietly said afterwards, "the fish make it easy."

And sometimes they don't. Later that day Bob would part the leaves of a shrub thirty feet above the river on a wooded bluff overlooking a boulder-strewn run. Through the branches, exactly in the spot where he knew it would be, was the biggest brown trout I've ever laid my eyes upon—in *or* out of a river. He estimated its size at well over ten pounds. It hung in the current like a misplaced steelhead, and instinctively I knew this was Bob's fish. I didn't even bother asking to take a stab at it, which would have been like, say, asking your dentist if you could wing it on the next patient.

The wind was howling again by this time, and Bob slipped below and took his turn at waiting out the gust. I watched solemnly and gave directions from above. At just the right moment a great loop of line landed the nymph slightly behind and to one side of the trout. The great fish lay perfectly still, then pensively drifted toward a large midstream lie, which I telegraphed to Bob.

"That's it," he said. "He's locked up. He always moves to the same spot when he's scared." It struck me then that Bob must have cast to this fish often enough to figure out its routine, but I decided that now wasn't the best time to broach the subject.

By day's end we'd each released a few fish and lost a few more—a good day by New Zealand backcountry standards. The largest was seven-and-a-half pounds. That night a large contingent from the Auckland Tramping Club straggled in while we dined on pepper steak, oysters, and chocolate biscuits, all washed down with white wine and cold beer courtesy of the Land Rover and a cooler. "You're not going to eat steak in front of us?" half-joked a club member preparing the usual backpackers' fare of freeze-dried pasta.

"No," Bob replied. "We'll turn our backs."

The next weekend we rejoined Steve in hopes of fishing on the West Coast around the Lake Brunner area. But it was pouring rain, the water was up, and the rivers were off. "I think I'm going to give it a go anyway," Steve said. He was standing in front of a dart board at the Ikamatua pub, staring blankly at the rivulets of water cascading off the deck. The water running off the deck had obviously tapped a buried emotion, and Steve was determined to go fishing.

"Don't be a fool, Smithy," Bob replied. "Look, it's no use. Why don't we all just order another jug and make the best of a bad situation?" You'll forgive me if my chronology is off, but in an inebriated order of events, this is what followed: we went to Blackball; we went to the pub; we ordered three jugs; seven hours later we ordered three more jugs; Steve began nodding in agreement; I staggered up the street to the artist's colony we called home for the night; an hour later Bob and Steve woke me up, chanting a mantra.

The next day they dropped me off at the intersection of two highways to hitch north. Their motto kept knocking about in my head, which given the circumstances, hurt like hell:

When the wind is in the north—
It's time to venture forth
When the wind is in the west—
Do not leave the nest
When the wind is in the south—
The beer is in the mouth
When the wind is in the east—
That's when you'll get the beast.

I received a letter from Bob a couple of months later. He'd begun plans to start guiding out of Arthur's Pass, a small town in the mountains northwest of Christchurch. He'd also shot a small stag during the first fifteen minutes of a twenty-one-day hunting trip, then hadn't seen another deer for the next three weeks.

"Shit happens when you party naked," he wrote, and I still don't know whether he culled the line from a book or made it up himself. I still don't know what it means, either.

The letter went on to say that he'd hooked that huge brown trout at the bottom of the bluff. He used a 4x tippet and a small nymph. "I lost him," he wrote. "I was so pissed off I almost rolled in the river myself." He didn't say if he laughed about it afterwards, but I have a feeling he did.

When Kiwis start talking about pigs, take note. Listen carefully, with the same attentiveness you'd oblige an Alaskan outfitter talking about grizzlies. New Zealand pigs are no laughing matter. Not once you've seen one or two of the wild boar heads mounted in a pub. In Murchison, a quaint little South Island town on the banks of the world-famous Buller River, there are pig heads hideous enough to make you forget about beer—to make you forget about the fabulous fish-and-chips and the two girls leaning over the pool table in halter tops.

Their flat snouts (I'm talking about the pigs now) are the size of small plates, their heads as big as a black bear's. The ivory tusks sticking out of their jaws could renovate a piano. Those aren't pigs, I thought to myself the first time I saw them. They're monsters!

New Zealand's wild pigs (Australia has them, too), which grow to well over 300 pounds, were introduced by English explorer Captain James Cook in 1774 as a source of food for settlers. Ironically, although the pigs ran rampant over Europe several centuries ago, today their numbers are dwindling there and the pigs are extinct over much of their original range.

However, that's not the case in New Zealand, and since the pigs aren't native and, like the wombats in Oz, not highly regarded, it's not surprising that the Kiwis get such a kick out of shooting them.

"Experience the thrill of the hunt," began one brochure I picked up in Murchison. It went on to say that for $150 (Kiwi), the hunter would be treated to "an adventure with dogs and knives under 'fair-chase' conditions (i.e., no fencing, feeding, or artificial stocking of pigs)." I gather the knives are for finishing off the cornered beasts in chivalrous fashion, but I'm only guessing. I was tempted to give it a go—mainly to say I'd done it and all that—but the next item on the brochure talked me out of it.

Under the heading "Varmint Hunting," the operators had written the following: "With rifle and spotlight, try your luck at a red eyed possum glowing in the dark, or bag yourself a bobtail flitting through the undergrowth."

I hunt, but the idea of spotlighting possums and rabbits and blasting them had never occurred to me. New Zealand pigs are no laughing matter, and neither is any hunter who spotlights game, no matter what their origins.

FIRST IMPRESSIONS

The three of us, positioned single file but staggered like a flight of geese, were skulking along the bank of a rushing freestone stream near Arthur's Pass. Stepping gingerly from rock to rock, Bob and Steve scrutinized the water with osprey-like intensity. I followed, trying more or less to be involved, but feeling, to be frank about it, more like a burr they'd picked up along the way.

"Always keep your rod pointing backwards, away from the water," Bob instructed, his eyes never leaving the river. Sheepishly, I flipped the cork grip around in my hand.

"It takes some getting used to, but it's important to keep looking in the water and not at your feet," Bob said. I followed his advice, tripped on a boulder, and almost knocked Bob and Steve over like a pair of dominoes. The sky was leaden and a fine mist swirled down between the mountaintops: I convinced myself there was no way we were going to spot a fish in the flat light. We'd been walking along the bank at least twenty minutes, covering maybe two hundred yards, when the procession ground to a halt.

"What's up, Smithy?" Bob asked Steve. "See something?"

"Maybe," Steve replied. "I've got an impression."

"A *what*?" I interjected, not sure if I'd heard him correctly.

"An impression," Bob answered. "Sometimes Smithy thinks he sees a fish but isn't sure. He calls it an impression." Bob asked Steve to show him the spot, and they stared at it, the two of them, like necromancers trying to summon a fish from Hades.

"Yeah," said Bob, "it's a fish all right." Apparently, they'd seen it move. I was still trying to penetrate the metallic sheen on the water and make out the riverbed below. And then I saw it, too, a dark shadow, more illusion than substance. I couldn't believe that Steve had picked the fish out in the middle of all that rushing water and blinding glare. A shadow. An *impression!* Christ.

Traveling to New Zealand to fish blind is like going to a whorehouse with empty pockets. In fact, New Zealand is one of the few angling destinations in the world where the combination of limpid water and large fish make sight fishing—insofar as the mountainous areas are concerned—the norm rather than the exception. The truth is that sight fishing is also one of the most exhilarating sensations that flyfishing has to offer. Anyone who's cast to a rising fish is familiar with the added thrill of knowing where the trout is holding. But when you can actually *see* the trout finning in the water like a slumbering torpedo, the thrill is amplified to the point of delirium.

Weather is everything while sight fishing. Other things to consider are the time of day, position of the sun relative to the water, the color of the riverbed, and the color of the water itself. The aquamarine pools of the North Island's upper Ngaruroro and Rangitikei rivers, for instance, lend themselves to spotting fish. There were times on the Ngaruroro when I'd lean over a bluff fifty feet above the river and spot fish as easily as you'd pick out sunbathers sprawled along a beach. On the other hand, while the nearby upper Mohaka River is just as clear, I had trouble spotting fish over much of its length because of the gold-colored, sculpted lava formations lining the stream bottom.

Almost without exception, the best sight fishing occurs under sunny skies or a very thin haze. That's assuming, of course, that the angler is able to position himself so that the sun is at his back. Midday is best, because the sun's rays strike the water at a more direct angle and surface reflection is kept to a minimum. Generally, sight fishing becomes more difficult later in the afternoon, when shadows lengthen and the glare intensifies. For this reason, Kiwis weaned on spotting fish rarely angle much past supper or much before mid-morning. (If only we North Americans, accustomed to driving at night to be at streamside come first light, could be so civilized.)

One of the obvious benefits to fishing by banker's hours is that you'll rarely miss breakfast. I swallowed an ample portion of bacon and eggs one morning before setting out to fish the Oreti River near the small town of Mossburn on the South Island. The Oreti reminded me a lot of the Bow River south of Calgary. Up to several hundred yards wide in places, it wound over gravel floodplains between brush-covered islands, the clear water flowing along distinctly braided channels. Tall prairie grass lined the banks, interrupted in places by clothes-catching, thorny matagouri bushes. Also known as wild Irishman, the matagouri's thorns were used by Maoris for tattooing. It occurred to me more than once that a crooked matagouri thorn might have made a decent makeshift fish hook in a tight situation.

The day started beautifully; the sun directly overhead, the wind slight, the brown trout, as Bob was wont to say, "on the feed." I caught and released several nice fish, but about noon the clouds started rolling in and the sight fishing became increasingly difficult. The problem under such conditions is that the river takes on the same gray hue as the sky, and even with polarized glasses on, seeing into the water is like trying to look through a cupboard door.

Ironically, when it comes to sight fishing, the actions of the fish itself go a long way toward determining its fate. A motionless fish is more difficult to spot than a trout on the move. Of course, the same axiom applies to most of the so-called blood sports: a running deer is sure to draw more attention as well, as is a pheasant bolting down an irrigation ditch. Similarly, a trout feeding just beneath the surface—especially in deeper water—is much more visible. Anglers can normally spot a fish like that from well downstream if they approach carefully.

Should the same fish decide to take up a deeper feeding position, however, spotting it will become that much more challenging. You may not glimpse a trout like that until you're almost beside it, and by then it's usually too late. If, by chance, the trout hasn't spooked, the only thing to do is to slowly . . . *slowly* . . . retrace your steps backwards until you're once again in good casting position well behind the fish. Contrary to popular theory extolling a trout's incredible vision, you'll be amazed how many fish you'll walk alongside and stare in an eyeball before dropping back down and hooking them several minutes later.

Trout holding on the very bottom of the streambed are a different story altogether. There's a segment in the movie *Predator* in which a team of specially trained soldiers, led by none other than Arnold Schwarzenegger, discover they're being stalked by an alien in a Central American jungle. The alien is able to camouflage itself at will, shimmering in and out of sight and even becoming transparent like an oversized camera lens. Just so you get the complete picture, the alien-*cum*-camera lens leaps from tree to tree, swinging like Tarzan through the thick jungle foliage.

All things considered, *Predator* is a pretty good movie. But it's an even better instructional video on the sort of thing anglers can expect trying to spot trout lying on the bottom of a river. The trout aren't apt to swing from tree to tree, of course, but nature provided them with similar camouflage, the same sort of spectral translucency. It's difficult to describe, really, but instead of looking for something that *is,* the angler is basically looking for something that *isn't:* an absence of color; something missing on the riverbed; a shadow that shouldn't be there. You can stare at one of Steve's "impressions" for minutes, but just as often as not, you're still not absolutely certain there's a fish there until it sweeps its tail or swings to take a nymph before reassuming its ghostly lie.

Compounding matters is the fact that, over time, brown trout are very good at taking on the coloration of their surroundings. If, for instance, a trout has spent its life drifting over golden cobblestones, it's liable to be a beautiful shade of amber. Likewise, the same species of trout inhabiting mountainous gravel streams can be as lustrous as silver salmon.

Just how invisible trout can get became clear to me one afternoon while walking slowly (there's that word again) along the bank of the Travers River on the South Island. It was overcast; spotting fish was tricky. The river had picked up speed, tumbling over a boulder-strewn run, and I eyeballed the pockets on the downstream side of each rock for any sign of fin or tail. I'd just about covered the section when a huge fish rose through a patch of broken water, gulped something or other and disappeared again, leaving the image of an orangish tail flapping in my mind.

I froze, scanning the bottom to try and spot the brown trout lying there. Nothing. It rose again. Still nothing. It must have been holding in the slack water behind the rock, but the trout evaded all my attempts to see it. When I finally got around to tossing a nymph its way, the trout spooked, racing across the river. Judging from where it bolted, I'd been staring at its back the whole time.

No matter how tough the sight fishing, there are still a few things the Down Under flyfisher can do to increase his chances of catching a trout. Getting dressed in the morning is a good place to start. If you're going to be fishing along an open, graveled riverbed, Bob advises khaki. In other words, dress like a stone. The same dust-colored wardrobe will do quite nicely along rivers and lakes lined by prairie grass.

If, on the other hand, you're going to be fishing along bushy streams winding through a rainforest, the idea isn't to look like a stone, but a tree. Green's the answer here. That's all you'll need—green and khaki. You'll also get away with wearing blue, but don't be fooled by the fluorescent fleece pullovers, Day-Glo caps, and vermilion fishing vests being peddled by the Madison Avenue crowd. Gear like that may look great on film, but it really has no place in a serious flyfisher's closet. And that's not just a Down Under flyfisher's closet, either. I used to wear all sorts of brightly colored clothes when I fished back home, but no more. The way I see it, why handicap yourself? After all, you wouldn't go duck hunting in blaze orange, would you?

Once you've settled on a basic Down Under fishing wardrobe, it's time to consider the accessories. Polarized sunglasses are a must, preferably with wrap-around lenses that shield the sides of your eyes as well. Not only will these help you spot fish, they'll also keep your eyes from getting fried in the process. A wide-brimmed hat with a dark underside is also a good idea. Don't bother with anything loose fitting, however. Those infamous South Island winds will quickly carry a hat like that away, which may explain why you won't see too many anglers wearing baseball caps along the exposed rivers there. The best bet is to get something with a chin strap and a toggle and then not worry about looking like a four-year-old contestant at the local mutton-busting competition.

If there's one thing I brought to New Zealand that I wished I had not, it's chest waders. No doubt some will find them useful, and they *do* come in handy if you're planning to wade out into the big lakes or rivers to fish, but I found they took up too much space in my backpack and weren't necessary. I waded wet ninety-five percent of the time, either with bare legs and shorts, shorts with running tights underneath (to thwart the sandflies), or if it was cold and windy, in shorts with nylon wind pants overtop. The mountainous Kiwi streams are as cold as water gets, but if you're sight fishing correctly and staying out of the water as much as possible, you won't be submerged long enough to get chilled.

For the same reason, New Zealand-bound anglers should probably leave their felt-soled wading boots at home, too. The best idea is to wait until you fly to Christchurch or Auckland, search out one of the larger outdoor clothing stores, and pick yourself up a pair of gum rubber, lace-up Buller boots. These ankle-high, black beauties are equally at home in the water or out, and the only regret I have involving Buller boots is that I didn't bring a spare pair back to Canada with me when I flew out of Auckland at trip's end. Besides, Buller boots are something of a status symbol among Kiwi anglers. Who knows, they might even lead to a stubby or two.

If there's one thing I didn't bring to New Zealand that I'm glad I didn't, it's a small wooden landing net. Don't get me wrong: these are beautiful nets. But when chances are good that you'll be hoisting a seven- or eight-pound trout out of the water, once again, why handicap yourself? I found the best net I've ever owned in a small South Island shop, a bombproof, metal collapsible model that fits perfectly next to my rod tube on the side of my backpack. While fishing, I angle it diagonally in the pocket on the back of my vest like a quiver, doing the zipper up enough to hold it in place. Positioned this way, it's easy to reach back, pull it out, and snap the net in place without losing a beat.

The only thing wrong with my net is that it doesn't have a built-in scale. As you'll recall, Bob had one like that; a fancy job that he held in the air by the handle to see how much the fish weighed. The only thing wrong with his net was that it didn't collapse. It would be nice to have the best of both net worlds, but I have yet to find a collapsible net with a built-in scale. Such is life.

Strangely enough, another angling accessory that you'll be hard pressed to find Down Under is the float tube. I saw more in shops than I did on the water, and I didn't exactly see a lot of them in shops. By contrast, there's not a summer day on Montana's Blackfeet Reservation that you won't see dozens, if not hundreds, of belly boats scattered across the lakes like lily pads. But the float tube phenomenon just doesn't seem to have caught on Down Under.

Of course, there are exceptions. I met a nice kid at Pine Tier Lagoon in Tasmania who spoke about his float tube as if it was the Second Coming. A thoughtful youth, he'd equipped his girlfriend with a float tube as well. She didn't fish much but seemed to get a kick out of her belly boat nonetheless, circling her mate like a bird engaged in a bizarre courtship ritual. Watching the two of them set out across the lake at sunset was like watching the loons frolic in *On Golden Pond*, another movie anglers should see if only to learn how *not* to drive a boat.

In an ideal world and on an ideal Down Under fishing trip, an overseas angler would show up with three or four of his favorite fly rods and a sack-full of reel and spool combinations. As a matter of fact, that approach is entirely feasible for someone staying in a central lodge or hotel who doesn't have to worry about carting his gear (including the kitchen sink) everywhere he goes. Under such circumstances, I'd bring everything from a three- to an eight-weight and be prepared to catch anything from an eight-inch rainbow to a ten-pound brown.

But place an internal frame pack on someone's back with just enough room for a four-piece travel rod in a side pocket, and things get dicey. I fished over small streams on calm mornings when a three-weight would have been perfect. Other times, maybe even later that same day, I fished over sprawling lakes in gale-force winds when a harpoon wouldn't have been out of the question. Compromising,

I carried a nine-foot six-weight. If I could do it all over again, I might opt for more firepower and choose a seven-weight. For some reason or other, the days when gale-force winds drove me screaming in defeat seemed to outnumber the calm mornings, and be it in war or in fly-fishing, I'd rather be over-armed than outgunned.

I've already noted that abusing "Yanks," either in front of their faces or behind their backs, seems to be something of a pastime Down Under. The fact that Americans are occasionally referred to as "seppos" (the reference is to septic tanks) probably says it all.

On New Zealand's South Island, I met a Canadian brother and sister duo who swore that they'd tripled their hitching success by sewing large Maple Leafs onto their backpacks. In fact, according to the pair, several Kiwis told them outright that if they had sewn the Stars and Stripes onto their packs instead, the drivers wouldn't have stopped. I often asked Kiwis and Aussies why Yanks get the bum rap down there. Their responses varied, but two themes repeatedly emerged: first, Yanks have a worldwide reputation of butting in where they're not wanted; second, Yanks are the most overbearing, pompous, egotistical bunch on earth. The two themes, people explained, generally went hand in hand.

Yank anglers often got the bum rap, too. The exclusive New Zealand flyfishing lodges were only too eager to throw their doors open for wealthy Americans, but out on the water or in the pubs, behind their clients' backs, the Kiwi guides took enough shots at Yanks to knock down a road-full of country signs.

I have no doubt a lot of this was due to envy. Most of the Kiwi guides are forced to take off-season work to make ends meet each year, and in a country where unemployment tops sixty percent in some districts, any Yank who can afford to charter a helicopter each day for a month is bound to rub some people the wrong way.

No doubt a lot of the friction is due to the nature of the New Zealand fishing as well. More than once I heard Yanks complaining that on a so-called "good" day they'd only caught half-a-dozen fish. It didn't seem to matter that any one of those fish would have bettered anything they'd caught in the U.S. in the last five years. As I've said, flyrodders expecting non-stop action on New Zealand waters will surely be disappointed.

Then again, in the words of American author Thomas McGuane, "What is emphatic in angling is made so by the long silences—the unproductive periods." Nowhere does that emphasis manifest itself as it does in New Zealand.

THE YELLOW HOUSE

Imagine, if you will, a flyrodder, carefully making his way up an isolated river valley in electric blue lycra tights. The tights are supposed to thwart the dreaded sandfly swarms, and they do; the tiny flies, it turns out, can't bite through the thin fabric.

The tights are comfortable, quick drying, and—well, it doesn't really matter if the flyfisher looks like a geek, because there is nobody along the Travers River to tell him so. He is alone, hopping from rock to rock, wading from pool to pool, catching fish . . . playing Baryshnikov in a piscine *pas de deux*.

Then the bees show up. Bumblebees. Big bloody buzzing bastards. The tights, you see (he finds this out later, in a pub, when he isn't wearing tights), are the same color as a certain preferred alpine wildflower. The bees, apparently unconcerned that this flower is walking along the shore with a fly rod in its hand, do their best to pollinate the tights.

The first few bother the heck out of him. He's setting up to cast, stripping line from the reel, pulling the leader through the guides, when a dark object the size of a small stone lights on the tights. He brushes a bee off, swats a few, too. Then, recalling a previous run-in with wasps along the same river a week earlier, remembers a maxim etched into his mind since childhood: *a bee won't sting you if you leave it alone*. It's all he can stand, but the angler relents and lets the bees play airplane on his landing strips. They crawl around, satisfy themselves that he doesn't photosynthesize, then fly off. Sometimes he hosts two or three at the same time. He keeps wearing the tights because, he figures, the bees are still preferable to the sandflies.

But before long the bees begin to take certain liberties that he can't tolerate. When they start roaming around on his crotch, for instance, it puts a certain strain on the—er, relationship. He finds it impossible to lay out fifty feet of line with a bee crawling over his testicles. His fishing suffers; the tights come off; the sandflies hold sway.

I was reminded of those bees when, a few nights later, three Danish women tramping up the river valley showed up at the backcountry hut to spend the night. Danes being the generally unabashed lot that they are, the women proceeded to strip down to their underwear in the humid hut, the flickering candles throwing parabolic shadows against the timber walls. My mind raced, my crotch tingled. Bees again. Birds. I'd like to say that we talked about sex—about three women and one man and the myriad possibilities thereof—but we didn't. We talked about politics. So much for pollination.

The Travers River valley is the Yellow Brick Road of New Zealand trout fishing. There's no telling who (or what) you'll encounter there. Bumblebees. Danish women. Use your imagination. The Yellow Brick Road, naturally, begins at the Yellow House, a homey hostel at St. Arnaud run by one of the South Island's best-known flyfishing guides, David Moate. Like so many other guides I've met, David has a pair of intense, soulful eyes set amidst a tangle of crow's feet. I've heard eyes like that described as laughing eyes, and there's usually a smile on David's face, too. Despite being on the near edge of middle age, David has freckled cheeks and a brown mop of hair that make him look, to be honest, like a grown-up version of Opie off *The Andy Griffith Show*. He and his wife live next to the hostel in a Spartan bungalow, and Scott, their spaniel, lives in the backyard in a modest shack of his own. David wanted to call the dog Sage, but apparently his wife prefers a slower rod.

Anyway, the hostel is yellow. Not earth-tone yellow or golden yellow, but *yellow* yellow—like a lemon, like a field of canola. There's a long list of reasons why the Moates painted the hostel yellow. The list is nailed to the wall just inside the back porch. Basically the list says that the building is yellow because yellow is a bright color that makes people happy. As a flyfisher, of course, I've always associated yellow with the color the leaves turn about a month before the end of another season, which doesn't make me very happy at all.

Not far from the Yellow House there's a pretty good pub, and not far from the pub there's a lake called Rotoiti. That's the circuitous route I took the afternoon I set off for the Travers River valley from St. Arnaud. You can walk for about three hours along Rotoiti's east shore to where the river dumps into the south end of the lake, or if you're prone to occasional laziness like me, you can walk up to the friendly man driving the water taxi, hand him the same amount of money you'd spend on a good college football ticket, and take the easy way in. I'd decided, largely due to David's prompting, to spend a week fishing up the Travers, slowly working my way upstream until the trout and the backcountry huts petered out, both at about the same time. Actually, it was my second go at the Travers: my trip a week earlier had ended with that unfortunate wasp incident. But armed with my adrenaline syringe and determined to climb back on the horse, I wasn't about to let the wasps—or those pesky bumblebees—have the last say.

A popular trail parallels the Travers for most of its length, and I found the best way to fish was to divide the river into segments and tackle a different reach each day. By tramping upstream from one hut to the next every second or third morning, an angler can fish the entire river this way and see an awful lot of countryside to boot.

On the first morning my sleeping bag started beeping. When I realized it was the watch on my wrist, I crawled out, lit a candle, and contemplated crawling right back in again. Frankly, I've never been a morning person. I have a like-minded buddy who claims that he doesn't mind waking up early as long as it's to hunt, ski, fish, or have sex. Each to his own, I guess.

Because I was sight fishing, I waited until the sun had cleared the horizon before setting out. The river braided into two or three channels before entering the lake; I chose to walk up the nearest one. It was small, clear, and more like a stream than a river. The grassy banks were heavily undercut, and I carefully scrutinized the first deep pool I came to. It had the translucent quality of a gemstone, and through the pale blue shimmering depths I barely saw the outline of a nice trout lying on the gravel bottom. The cast was an awkward one, backhanded, and the trout spooked when the line and nymph failed to straighten and fell in a heap on the water.

I spotted the second fish just around the next bend. I had to stare at the dark object lying in about a foot of water a long time before convincing myself that it was indeed a trout and not an underwater appendage of one of several tree branches lodged in the river bottom. I still hadn't entirely convinced myself of its authenticity when, with a deft sweep of its tail, the fish darted to the side, consumed a food item, and quickly returned to its former lie. Had I chosen that moment to admire my fly rod's pleasing color in the morning sun or to have picked some grit from the corner of my eye, I'm sure I would have missed the episode entirely.

Comfortable in the assurance that I was casting to a trout and not a log, I tied a size 14 cream caddis to a 4x tippet and eased myself over the bank and onto a small gravel bar cutting across the width of the channel. While I preferred to stay out of the water while sight fishing, the banks were cluttered with tall grass and shrubs and the gravel bar looked too inviting to pass up. Although I hadn't seen the trout take a dry fly, I figured the water in the run where it was holding was shallow and clear enough that it was bound to notice anything floating on the surface.

The line whistled through the air, the bushy fly reached terminal velocity, and the presentation went off without a hitch. Bobbing gently on the water, the artificial was eclipsed by a dark shadow and then it was gone. I struck. The fish was on. It tore upstream and lunged clear of the water, a brown trout, its broad flank hanging in the air like a buttery crescent moon, shining and brilliant. The fish made several runs both upstream and down. When it had tired and rolled onto its side, I grabbed the collapsible net from the pocket at the back of my vest, flipped it open, and swept the green twine toward the trout. Just as it teetered on the brink of capture, the fish flopped onto the wrong side of the net, the hook came free, and the trout and I stared at one another for an excruciatingly long moment. I lunged forward and tried to swipe it out of the river grizzly style, but the fish had just enough energy to shimmy away with the current.

I eventually caught a few fish that day. And the next. And the day after that. But for all of the fish and all of the fishing, the thing I remember most is the valley itself; the exquisite beauty of towering beech trees trailing streamers of diaphanous moss; the smell of dank earth; tendrils of mist spiraling skyward off the river as my cold fingers threaded the tippet through the eye of the day's first hook; the afternoon clouds swirling around peaks as gray as a grandfather's beard.

There were times on the Travers River when everything came together for me as a flyfisher. The physical act of casting was reduced to a mental state of being. All very Zen-like. All very proper. I didn't worry about line control, didn't remind myself to keep my wrist straight. I'd picture things in my mind, then see them happen a moment later. The fishing was becoming reflexive, rehearsed a thousand times and yet unorchestrated. It happens to a flyrodder every now and then, and when it does, it's a moment to be cherished, because something in the back of your mind keeps telling you that by next week (maybe even by later that same afternoon) you'll be casting figure-eights again and leaving far too many flies in the bankside shrubbery.

More often than not that week the wind was at my back, blowing upstream. Because the Travers flows in a northerly direction and the summer winds often blow out of the northwest, the river is, unlike many of the South Island's freestone streams, forgiving water. That's not to say that it's *easy* water, but rather that it's the sort of river where you usually won't have to worry about getting a fifteen-foot leader to turn over into a twenty-mile-per-hour wind.

The farther I worked up the river, naturally, the smaller it got. The beech trees were more liable to abut the water's edge. The narrow runs were rocky and fish were more difficult to spot in the roily current. The distances between sighted fish became greater. And yet, as with any other journey to a river's headwaters, I felt a primal urge to press on, a feeling that the next step could send me back ten thousand years, or ten million. There's a Holy Grail optimism to a headwaters trip—the knowledge that somewhere in the constricted froth is a trout worthy of the crusade. It may be difficult to locate, you tell yourself, but if and when you do, it's yours for the taking. Yours alone.

I located my Holy Grail downstream of the John Tait Hut. It lay beneath an awkward beech bough against the far bank, appearing, at first, like an impossible fish to catch. On the side of the river where I was standing, a wayward channel re-entered the main current, fanning out and spilling diagonally for about twenty-five yards over a shallow gravel fan. Ironically, I'd almost walked right past the big trout, failing to notice it in the shadowy water before the flick of its tail wrested my attention from trying to navigate the slippery streambed. I froze, amazed that the fish hadn't spotted me. I reasoned that it must have been holding too deeply to see my silhouette through the water, which thankfully was bubbling and churning where the two currents came together.

Moving slowly to avoid detection, I made the only cast I could, sidearming the fly a few feet in front of the overhanging branch and letting the diagonal current sweep the line and leader across the main channel. A miniature whirlpool quickly tugged the yarn strike indicator beneath the surface. Switching my gaze to the fish, I instinctively set the hook when I saw it dart sideways. The line bellied as the faster current swept it downstream, and I figured I'd missed the fish for sure. No sooner did I start reeling in, however, than the remaining line straightened with a *twang* and the hooked trout shot downstream, the frenzied reel screeching like a bandsaw.

Since there were no pools to speak of and the trout seemed determined to locate the lake, I really had no choice but to run along the bank and put as much pressure as I dared on the taut 3x tippet. Finally the fish stopped and turned upstream. I reached across my right shoulder with my left hand to pull the net from its vest-pocket sheath. During the process, a strap gave out on my day pack and it tumbled to the ground with a thud. The trout took advantage of the ensuing confusion to turn around and take off downstream again. I followed, of course, leaving the pack where it lay and fully expecting the strained leader to snap like a worn guitar string. Somehow it held. Somehow the trout toppled into the right side of the net I slipped under its obese girth, head and tail protruding as the mesh stretched to accommodate the twenty-five-inch, silver-flanked horseshoe.

I released the prize and howled like a moonstruck coyote. At nothing. At everything. *Ouooooooo . . . woooo!* Then, retrieving my day pack, I found a large rock and sat down to savor the moment and the sweet taste of apricot jam on rye crackers. My hands were still shaking when I picked up the knife.

Forthwith, I'd like to point out that many flyrodders wouldn't be satisfied with catching three, four, maybe five trout a day, no matter what the size. Those numbers suited me just fine, however. Even back in Canada, I've never fished for totals—just for the overall experience of fishing. I started to think of the New Zealand trout the same way that a hunter may think of deer. It's great just to sight a big buck; getting a shot at one is a bonus and bagging it euphoric. And, regulations notwithstanding, unless you own a game farm or do your shooting from a helicopter, you don't just go around bagging a dozen trophy bucks a day, no matter who you are. Every time I try to explain New Zealand sight fishing to someone, the hunting analogy inevitably resurfaces. As with hunting, the New Zealand weather (which plays such a key role in sight fishing) could make or break a trip there.

It was raining outside—pouring—and a motley collection of international trampers were gathered in the sitting room at the Yellow House. A blonde German woman was taking advantage of the weather to peddle woven wristbands and anklets, and sales were brisk. Several people were writing letters or postcards. A few were reading. David Moate walked into the room with an armload of firewood and tossed a couple of pieces into the stove.

"That should help take some of the chill off the afternoon," he said, but three or four of us had our own solution. We headed for the pub. Beer, another German surmised, beat wood anytime. Even the ever-reliable suds, however, couldn't wash away a bad case of the flyfishing blues. The rain fell long and hard enough to put the rivers in flood for at least another day; the water flowed out of the mountains like bean with bacon soup. Great to dip bread in, lousy for spotting fish.

The rain had tapered to a bothersome drizzle by the time I hitched a ride to the Lake Rotoroa boat launch. Rotoroa lies across the Travers mountain range from Rotoiti and isn't to be confused with Lake

Rotorua, one of the North Island's most popular fishing destinations. Trampers with lungs to spare can hike from one lake to another via several alpine passes. Another option is to tramp up the Travers River, cross over the scenic Travers Saddle, and descend to the upper Sabine River. The Sabine, unlike the Travers, offers the angler rainbow trout along with the browns.

Because the mountains were smothered in cloud, I'd decided to forsake the alpine passes and take another water taxi up Lake Rotoroa. A bigger lake than Rotoiti, the tramp up Rotoroa's east shore to the Sabine Hut at the south end of the lake takes at least five hours. Another two hours brings a tramper around to the southwest corner of the lake, where the D'Urville River empties into Rotoroa on the other side of the Mahanga mountain range from the Sabine. If all of this is starting to sound a tad confusing, just picture three of the South Island's most highly touted freestone rivers flowing roughly parallel to each other into two lakes and you'll know all you really need to.

I was trying to take it all in while I waited for the boat driver, a former guide at the pricey Rotoroa Lodge, to meet me at the dock. The rain had stopped; the lake's surface was leaden, as if it had been poured from a spigot and left to solidify. A couple of ducks flapped about noisily in the rushes. I kept expecting a fish to rise, but the surface was still. It was so quiet I could hear the rain water dripping off the beech leaves in the forest at my back.

Eventually the driver showed up, and we climbed into the boat. The ride took over half an hour, and he dropped me off at the Sabine Hut. It was crowded with waterlogged trampers, their wet clothes dangling like Christmas tree ornaments from the rafters and wire hangers. The hut was muggy that night; sleeping was difficult. The next morning we all went our separate ways. I decided to hike over to the D'Urville Hut to fish the river of the same name for two or three days.

Unfortunately, the D'Urville was off-color and unfishable. The rain had started falling again; it didn't peter out until the next morning. I spent the day in the hut, reading and updating my trip diary. That night it was clear and cold. I pushed the wooden table near the crackling pot-bellied stove and played solitaire until the candle and my eyes started giving out at about the same time.

The next day the water was clear enough to spot fish, but still slightly off-color. I worked my way well up the D'Urville without sighting anything, which was really frustrating after all the hype I'd heard about it being so good, maybe even better than the Travers. Finally I spotted a big brown trout circling in a strong backwater, but it was a tough cast and I put the fish down after trying in vain to entice it with a nymph.

Rather than work my way farther up the D'Urville (a mistake, I was later told, because some of the best flyfishing is up past Morgan Hut), I tramped back over to the Sabine the next morning to try my luck there. Following the track upstream, I noticed that the dark beech trunks beside the trail were covered in what looked like golden moss. At one point the trail steepened, and I reached out to grab a tree but instantly recoiled when it became obvious the moss was moving and making a strange humming sound. The trunk was coated in wasps. I took a quick look around and saw that all the other trunks were as well.

Weeks later, I realized the extent of the problem when I picked up a magazine and discovered, among other things, that wasps are unwelcome in the native beech forests of the northern South Island. The nasty pests aren't native to New Zealand, and their introduction some years ago is threatening native birds like the kaka, tui, and bellbird, which compete with the wasps for the succulent honey dew. Recognizing the problem and the risk to the indigenous species, the Department of Conservation is combating the wasps with poison-bait stations and the development of a parasite to attack wasps in their nests. Nonetheless, for all their vexatious habits, the wasps still haven't affected the trout fishing; unless, of course, an angler is unfortunate enough to step on a nest or lean against one of those perilous beech trees.

Of greater nuisance to me that day were the three flyrodders I encountered on the Sabine's prime stretch of water after I had hiked three hours to get there. It turned out that they'd thoroughly flogged the meadow section I'd so desperately wanted to fish, but they were nice enough guys and, being Kiwis, had at least as much, if not more right to be there as I did. Still, it's hard not to be pissed off at a time like that—I don't care how saintly you are. After chatting with them for a while I tried fishing, but the few fish I *did* spot scattered and the day (aside from the fact that it was great to be alive, and fishing without success still beats almost anything else in the world) was a bust.

So was the rest of the week. After making the long trudge back to the D'Urville Hut that evening, I leaned my fly rod against a tree and didn't give it another thought. The next day, when I bent over to pick up my rod, I realized that a disrespectful rodent had gnawed the colorful sheath off one or two feet of fly line. Not only that, the little bugger had taken bites out of the plastic handle on the reel as well. (I mentioned this later to a fellow at a fishing shop in Christchurch, and he had a good laugh about it, blaming the damage on a mouse.)

After all I'd been through, being disarmed by a mouse shouldn't have surprised me. Then it started raining again. I read and slept the days away in the hut, waiting for the water taxi, hoping against all odds for another trio of Danes to drop by. Danes that didn't give a damn about politics.

It's getting scary, this attraction to cricket. It started as forced exposure: blaring televisions, pub talk, the game of the week. Slowly, albeit unwillingly, it began to sink in. I began to recognize, for instance, a good spin bowler—not unlike a baseball pitcher with a wicked curve. The batsmen, I learned, are as varied as the length of time it takes to play a match. There are power hitters and there are control hitters. There are speedsters and there are those whose bellies betray the beer-drinking habits of their possessors. Again, just like baseball.

In fact, the similarities between baseball and cricket are many. In the beginning I thought all cricketers were wimps, second-rate baseball wannabees. Several things changed my mind. First, cricket fielders don't wear gloves. They catch a ball with the consistency of rolled concrete with their bare hands—a ball often traveling well over sixty miles per hour. Mostly, they do this without flinching. Second, unlike in baseball, a cricket batsman must be prepared to hit the ball over three hundred and sixty degrees. If the ball hits the wooden wicket directly behind him, he's out, but anywhere else on the circular field is fair game. In cricket, there's no such thing as a ball being fouled back into the opposing team's dugout.

Until I met Fife and Dave, I thought I was alone. I kept my cricket fancy to myself, saw myself as a North American oddball. Clearly, I'd been brainwashed. Then, like I said, I met Fife and Dave, two good ol' New Jersey boys reared on mom's apple pie and the limestone trout streams of the Appalachia. They didn't come any more American than Fife and Dave. The three of us had been hanging out and fishing together for a couple of days in a small town on New Zealand's South Island. The town's namesake, the Twizel River, had been generous. (The day before, I'd caught four large browns and rainbows—two of each—and a handful of smaller fish.) On our last day together, Fife looked at Dave at about six o'clock in the evening and suggested they start back to the A-frame where we were staying. There were fish rising everywhere.

"To watch the big game," Fife explained, noting my shocked expression.

"You mean . . ." I cleared my throat. "The cricket game?"

"*Yeah. We've sort of been getting into it.*" *He shuffled his feet and snipped the fly off the end of his tippet. I'm sure he expected me to laugh. A tirade. He got neither. Half an hour later we'd secured the best seats in front of the TV, cracked three cold tinnies, and sent North American manhood for a loop. Once, just once, I looked outside and wondered what those fish were up to.*

Then Pakistan came to bat.

A WEEK ON THE WORSLEY

In the distance, the twin outboard motors cut a retreating foamy swath through the Worsley Arm of Lake Te Anau. I'd just handed the boat driver $300 in New Zealand bills (about $175 American) for the forty-five-minute ride to my drop-off. If all went according to plan, he'd pick me up again in a week. Seven days on the edge of a rainforest in the middle of nowhere.

It occurred to me that this would be a really lousy time to develop acute appendicitis or discover a tumorous lump on the back of my head. You tell yourself such things are unlikely, but logic holds little sway at a moment like that. The boat rounded a bend on the horizon and disappeared. I was utterly, absolutely alone. There was ringing in my ears. I decided that maybe I should be getting paid for this, not vice versa.

The white sand beach seemed strangely out of place, but a quick jaunt down the shoreline in either direction showed the inconsistency didn't last for long. The sides of the cup-shaped arm where Worsley Stream tumbled into the lake were steep and unnavigable. Silver waterfalls plunged off high cliffs, and exotic green tree ferns clung precipitously to slate gray rock walls sprouting directly from the lake. The jungle was melded to the water like copper to a pot; it was obvious that escape along the lake shore was impossible. I was, in effect, trapped between a rainforest and a hard place. If there was any consolation, it was that Worsley Stream is reputed to be one of the best places in the world to fish for large brown and rainbow trout, and here it was, practically flowing over my toes. If one has to be incarcerated, then Worsley Stream is the flyfisher's prison of choice.

I hoisted my backpack and trudged the short distance to the Department of Conservation hut at the edge of the lake. The ubiquitous South Island sandflies were pleased to discover another warm body in their midst, and a sizable following was swept into the one-room, wooden hut with me during the brief act of opening and closing the door. A cast iron, pot-bellied stove with fancy scrollwork around the base sat in the middle of the unfinished wood floor. The far wall sported a row of two-tiered bunk beds with green foam mattresses, while the walls to either side featured broad counters to cook and store gear on. There were a couple of mildewy chairs and several empty wine bottles spouting melted-down candle stubs where the corks should have been. A push broom, broken axe, and thin strip of wire slung from the roof to hang wet clothes on rounded out the interior. It was Spartan but functional, crude but livable. It was home for a week.

It had been raining off and on for the past three days, but I decided to give the stream a look anyway and unpacked my rod. I threw on a light shell and headed off in the direction of Worsley Stream on a rough and overgrown trail blazed by man but maintained by beast. After about half a mile, the river—the Worsley is a stream in name alone—appeared through the trees on my left. I reached a small clearing and walked up to the bank, the drab, forest-stained water gouging away at the undercut beneath my feet then deflecting off the bank like a hockey puck off the boards. I took a step back.

The water itself was fishable, but the sky had that leaden hue that makes sight fishing impossible, so I decided to leave the rod in its brown cloth bag. Hearing the muffled roar characteristic of rapids, I walked a little farther up the river to investigate. It turned out that the sound was not rapids at all, but the Saint Mary's Falls plunging vertically over a gleaming precipice a few hundred yards above the confluence of Saint Creek and the Worsley. The forest was silent save the rushing water, and the incessant noise seemed intrusive until I reminded myself that it is timeless and I had been there five minutes.

Back at the hut I was greeted outside the door by four huge brown trout hanging from a stringer looped over a rafter, their gaping jaws and staring eyes covered in flies, their amber bellies neatly severed. Inside the door three burly looking Kiwis rose to greet me and introduced themselves as a team of sheep shearers out for a day's fishing. They'd just arrived by motorboat from the Clinton River, the next major drainage north into Lake Te Anau and the river which parallels, over much of its course, Fiordland National Park's world-famous Milford Track (a four-day mountain tramp advertised as "the finest walk in the world"). Tucked against the Tasman Sea in the southwest corner of the South Island, Fiordland is also a World Heritage Park—a special United Nation's designation—and, as I'd discover shortly, more than able to live up to its reputation as a world-class trout fishery. The *reason* the fishing is still so good is that access to most of the park is limited because of its remoteness and the ruggedness of the terrain. Only those anglers who can afford to hire float planes, helicopters, or, in the case of those rivers spilling into Lake Te Anau, boats find their way in. But access is only part of the story: this isn't the sort of place you'd take the family on a Sunday picnic. The biting sandfly swarms reduce the graceful art of flyfishing to something resembling a spasmodic dance step at an alternative music club. Insect repellent helps, but you can only smother yourself in so much DEET before starting to feel like a fly rod being varnished at the factory.

And then there's the weather. When the moisture-laden westerlies sweeping off the Tasman Sea rise to clear the coastal mountains, it rains. Over six *yards* a year. It rains and rains, and the rainforest, like a sponge, soaks away the moisture until there's nowhere else to put it. Then it floods. There are anglers who venture into Fiordland for a week and never assemble their rods. There are anglers who venture into Fiordland for a day and, trapped on the wrong side of a rising river, stumble out a week later.

The strange part about all this is that just sixty miles or so to the east, where the aforementioned Oreti and Mataura rivers meander down open, windswept valleys of rolling prairie grass and thorny matagouri scrub, things can get so dry that farmers beg for rain. Go figure.

That's where the trio of sheep shearers were from. The brown trout, the group leader explained, fell to dry flies and a filleting knife.

At this point I was tempted to preach a little catch-and-release, but my Down Under travels had already proven the futility (if not the outright danger) of this, so I kept my mouth shut. The trio asked me if I'd been fishing upstream and I said no, that I'd walked over to take a look at the river but passed, hoping for better weather and clearer water tomorrow. Because they were leaving first thing in the morning, they decided to give it a go and scrambled out the door with rods in hand.

So much for solitude. I fired up the white gas stove and threw a pack of instant noodles into a pot of boiling water. Every now and then I walked over to the hut's front window and stared out at the brown trout, half expecting them to be gone. Out of curiosity I measured the largest with the small tape I always keep in a lower vest pocket. It read twenty-seven inches. The dead fish were both disturbing and fascinating.

At dusk the anglers returned empty-handed. They'd seen lots of big fish, hooked a few, but landed none. We lit the pot-bellied stove to take the chill off the evening, and they offered me a cold beer. They talked about their sheep-shearing exploits, and we laughed freely. The kamikaze sandflies popped in the candle flames as heat lured them to false targets. Just before dark a kea, the large drab-colored New Zealand mountain parrot, took up residence outside the hut and welcomed the night with its noisome squawk. At bedtime we blew out the candles and crawled into our sleeping bags as the pungent smell of burnt wax wafted about the room.

The foul weather had disappeared overnight, and the morning was razor-fine and clear. I intended to tramp several miles upriver before starting to fish, so I packed a small lunch and brought along the rain gear just in case. The sheep shearers were still asleep when I left.

I started out on the same trail as the day before, but it soon deteriorated to little more than a sun-flecked tunnel through an almost impenetrable forest. The ancient beech trees were covered in moss, great clumps hanging down like curtains over a stage. Jagged ferns and vines grabbed like hands, and it was impossible to travel without breaking my rod down. Every now and then I came across a root ball big enough to be an obstacle or something dangling over the path that, by all appearances, connected to nothing. The ground was slick and the humidity was palpable, a living, breathing thing. I could suddenly see how Conrad's Kurtz could be sustained by this throbbing *Heart of Darkness.* A startled wood pigeon burst from cover—unseen—and a small gray-and-black fantail flitted from branch to branch, curiosity overcoming fear as it followed me along the path.

Finally I reached a point where the gravel fans along the river were accessible and wadeable, and as easily as walking through a door, I entered the sunlit streambed and left the gloomy rainforest behind. The water was so clear that judging the depth of a pool was guesswork: it might have been twelve feet deep, it might have been sixty. The river was a series of nice runs and pools, and before long I'd overtaken the last visitor and the only footprints in the sand at water's edge were my own. I started spotting fish immediately, large, dark shadows suspended from invisible strings slowly working them back and forth in a quest for underwater morsels.

One fish held on a tawny shallow just to the side of where a small cataract tumbled into the head of a pool. From the way it swung from side to side, I could tell it was taking nymphs on the eddy line where the faster current doubled back on itself. I tied a size 8 Hare & Copper to the end of the sixteen-foot leader, attached a small indicator about three feet from the fly, and began searching for a spot from which to launch my attack.

Fronds of golden toi (a feathery plant that looks like an oversized ostrich plume) hung out from the bank, and a canopy of overhanging beech boughs made an overhand cast impossible, so keeping a low profile, I scrambled across a series of submerged boulders until I was kneeling on an especially large rock in midstream. The trout was about thirty-five feet above me and still feeding regularly. Casting sidearmed, I managed to shoot the fly so that the indicator landed just to the side of the main current and rode a glassy boil toward the fish. My hand tensed on the rod, and the yarn darted beneath the surface as the trout accepted the offering. I snapped my arm back and the line tightened, but still nothing happened. The trout was motionless, stricken, but I sensed its power as if by mental telepathy.

Suddenly the line sliced across the water to the other side of the pool, my arm following like a pinwheel, and the great weight came to bear. I knew that if the trout decided to run downstream I'd be trapped helplessly atop the boulder, but the fish played by the rules and stayed within the ring, circling me like a young Muhammad Ali while I stood my ground and duked it out from my elevated perch. The New Zealand fishing videos showing anglers running two or three hundred yards downstream to fight trout are laughable in their absurdity, because almost every Kiwi guide will tell you that a large brown trout will rarely hop pools if the angler exerts enough pressure on the fish. An angler standing on a midstream rock playing circus ringmaster apparently doesn't make for good footage though, so the producers do things their way.

Finally, I was able to slip a net under the fish and take a hasty measurement. It was a brown trout, and it was twenty-six inches long. Probably about seven or eight pounds, olive-backed, and with a mouth big enough to swallow my reel. I held it in the water until it swam from under my hand, contrasting its departure with the dead fish back at the hut.

Several hours later the sun was still shining brightly, a rarity in this part of the world, when I saw a large tail rise and then sink slowly out of sight in a small lie about a dozen feet off the bank. It's amazing how often you'll spot a tail, a back, or a fin in New Zealand and nothing else. The eyes register a body part and then it's up to the mind to draw a composite. Brown trout or rainbow trout? Large or small? Real or imagined?

That particular tail was no figment—it was as perfectly outlined as a whale's tail breaking the surface of the ocean. I tied on a small nymph and cast to it. The tail surfaced again, this time propelling a hefty rainbow trying like hell to throw my bothersome fly from its mouth. It was the first rainbow I'd hooked in New Zealand, and after weeks of fighting browns, I immediately sensed the difference. The rainbow bucked and bolted like a wild rodeo mount, not at all like the steady, insistent pressure of a determined brown trout. It's as if, say, the air force has suddenly assigned you to fly an F-16 fighter after years spent in the cockpit of a B-52 bomber. The rainbow had a healthy lipstick-colored stripe and measured twenty-five inches. I caught another slightly smaller rainbow about an hour later and called it a day at three trout totaling seventy-five inches in length, or about half a foot taller than myself. The comparison felt good.

The river had dropped enough during the day that I was able to cross from gravel bar to gravel bar to work my way back to the hut. The sheep shearers and their dead fish were gone, but they'd left me a carton full of fresh spuds, onions, carrots, radishes, a loaf of bread, and a dozen eggs. It was welcome and the sort of surprise I'd come to expect of these gracious, laid-back people.

The only sounds that night were my own and those of an opossum scrambling about on the roof. Even in the middle of nowhere, the brush-tailed possum is impossible to escape. Introduced from Oz in 1858 in an attempt to start a fur industry (its dense coat is known as Adelaide chinchilla), the marsupial brush-tail has become one of the most destructive pests in the country, emerging at night to feed on native trees, birds' eggs, and even the small birds themselves. Ranging in color from golden to cream to black, the brush-tail looks like a cat-sized squirrel, and has adapted equally well to man's presence. It's a lot cuter than the American common opossum, which has a hairless tail and ears and a shabby grayish white coat.

Brush-tail possum fur still fetches a few dollars in most parts of New Zealand. Unfortunately, the traps used to catch them can't discriminate between the brush-tails and flightless birds like the kiwi, and the indigenous avifauna face yet another obstacle. My obstacle was trying to get to sleep while the possum continued to clamor about on the roof. I rubbed my toes against the nylon at the end of my sleeping bag, and curled them around a pinch of goose down to reaffirm my security. The light of a quarter moon swept across the floor, signifying a clear sky.

Miraculously, the weather during my trip had been perfect. The days had been sunny and the winds slight. Too perfect. I kept looking over my shoulder for a darkening horizon. It arrived on the fourth afternoon. Its name was Selwyn and it pulled up on the beach with a boat and a wife, announcing that it would be using the hut as a base for the next couple of weeks while it hunted red deer up the valley.

It's not often that I take an instant dislike to someone, but Selwyn was one of those people. He was a pompous, overbearing, transplanted Englishman. He ran around trying to look busy while doing absolutely nothing. I figured that if he were around at the turn-of-the-century, he was the sort of guy who would have imported those deer and moose to shoot on weekends before tea. And sure enough, Selwyn dragged a dose of bad weather in with him like a tender behind a yacht, and I sat the fifth day out, trapped in the hut while it drizzled outside. I tried my best to be polite. Selwyn bustled and his wife doted. So much for my solitude again.

The next morning it was sunny again and I couldn't get upriver fast enough. It hadn't rained enough to spoil the river, so I tramped three miles or so before starting to fish, planning to work my way up to the confluence of Worsley Stream and Castle River and then continue up the latter. It was the first week of March, early autumn in New Zealand, and the previous day's rain had dumped snow on the mountaintops. Very beautiful.

I hadn't been fishing long when I came to the nicest pool I'd ever seen in my life. It was long, at least a hundred yards, and mirror-smooth. At its head the current entered slowly, deflecting around a dozen or so ghostly submerged boulders that took the whip out of the whitewater. The arc of its tail wasn't unlike a dinosaur's, the water flowing over cobblestones sloping gently upwards until gravity seemed fooled and the current piled up against itself in a miniature weir. Walking along the treed far bank, I spotted seven trout lazily finning in the emerald water. Not one of them was under five pounds. Thankfully, a large gravel bar extended the length of the other bank, making casting easy. I told myself this pool should have been fished out. Who knows, maybe the helicopter pilots hadn't figured out a way to land there. One of the trout lying with its snout on a white rock in less than half a foot of water rose and took an insect. I tied on a size 14 Irresistible and hooked the fish on the first pass. It was that easy. The rainbow fought awkwardly, perhaps sedated by midday lethargy, and quickly came to net. It measured twenty-four inches. The other fish weren't fooled as readily as I worked my way up the pool, most just drifting off to the side after numerous casts to let me know they didn't appreciate my artificial game. At the pool's head I hooked and quickly lost a very big shadow that neatly severed my line against one of those huge submerged boulders. A nagging voice told me this was a "double-digit" trout, but again, who knows?

The pool where the Castle entered the Worsley was deep and foreboding. Strong eddies swung to either side and much of the cauldron was bounded by slab rock. It was intimidating and captivating: the former because deciding where to cast first was like deciding where to take your first step in a minefield, and the latter because you just knew there was a honking fifteen-pound brown lurking in the emerald depths. It was the first time since I'd been in New Zealand that I wished I'd had a sink-tip line (and a Silver Zonker), because I could almost picture that big brown sucking in a fake minnow like a wayward strand of spaghetti. *Slurp.* Because I had neither the sink-tip line nor the fly, I skipped the pool altogether. The thought of a fish that big stirring to take a dry fly or weighted nymph was too much for my resolve, too hard on the nerves. I figured there are some things that just aren't meant to be, and this was one of them.

That night our little hut party was joined by two kayakers who had also come over from the Clinton River. I went to hang my damp wading shorts and sweat-soaked top on the wire above the stove as usual, but it was full and I had to look elsewhere. Brad was a fireman from California staying with Penny, a friend and one of New Zealand's top triathletes. He'd been flyfishing for years. She was just learning. The three of us agreed to fish together the next day while Selwyn and Pat made plans for a week-long hunting and fishing excursion up the Castle River valley.

"How's the fishing been?" Brad asked.

"Good," I replied, but then, thinking it over, reservedly added, "but I guess it depends on what your definition of good is. I'm landing two or three nice fish a day and losing a few more. They're all big. I don't think I've even seen a fish in this river under four or five pounds."

"Sounds good enough to me," Brad said, and I knew we'd get along.

The next morning I decided at the last minute not to fish, but instead to concentrate on taking pictures with Brad and Penny as models. He had a peach-colored cap that I kidded him about, but to be honest, together with his pink fly line it made for good photos against the backdrop of green and brown earth tones and the blue sky. I felt a bit bad because the fish were especially spooky after I'd bombed them up the last few days, and he hooked just one trout all day.

Realizing the difficulties of catching fish here, Penny was mostly content to watch and periodically wander off to practice casting. Her loops were surprisingly tidy for someone starting out. Brad explained that she was a gifted athlete who just the previous week had finished in the top three in the Coast to Coast, a grueling international endurance race across the width of the South Island. Almost as an afterthought, he added that she was several months pregnant. After fishing upstream a few miles, the duo announced that they had to get going so they could kayak out and meet the *Tawera*, the passenger boat that ferries hikers daily from Te Anau Downs to Glade House and the start of the Milford Track.

"We hope you don't mind, but we're sort of in a hurry so we thought we'd run along the river back to the hut," Penny said, reaching into her day pack and pulling out a pair of all-terrain sneakers. We said our goodbyes, and I dumbfoundedly watched she and Brad hop from rock to rock, jog across a bend in the river, and vanish into the trees. I sat down and pulled an orange from *my* day pack, the juice sticky on my fingers and cool in my mouth. The sky was a washed-out tungsten blue, the beech trees on the slope across the river distorted in haze. I felt washed out, too.

Penny and Brad had packed and cleared out of the hut by the time I walked back. I wandered down to the beach, spotting them far offshore paddling like mad in their brightly colored kayaks to make their rendezvous. The hut was quiet again that night, but just before blowing out the candles I heard a single gunshot. Selwyn? It seemed too close. Maybe he hadn't gone as far as he said he would.

The next morning I ate a cold breakfast of oats and milk and gathered my things to make my own appointed rendezvous. The motorboat pulled up on the beach and I was happy to see the driver again. He glanced at Selwyn's beached boat under its canvas tarp and said it looked like I'd had company. Yes, I said, more company than I'd expected. I went to throw my backpack in the bow and there was a dead possum lying next to a rifle. The shot? Yes, the driver explained, he drove the forty-five minutes last night before dark, camped farther down the arm, and shot the possum with the aid of a spotlight. No doubt its red eyes had glowed in the dark.

When armchair anglers think of New Zealand trout, they think BIG. What they seem to be forgetting, or at least overlooking, is that even the biggest trout had a modest beginning. Storks don't deliver fish, they eat them.

So where are all the small New Zealand trout? Why can you walk for days up a mountain stream, spot dozens of fish, and not see one under three pounds? The explanations vary. One theory has it that the best spawning water in a river is usually well downstream from the headwaters, and juvenile fish wait there until they're bolder, larger, and at least two or three years old before swimming upstream. Jim Stelfox, an Alberta fisheries biologist and former Kiwi deer culler, says he's witnessed the same phenomenon during electroshocking surveys on Canadian mountain streams. (Anglers take note.)

In other instances, while smaller trout may be present, the anglers either aren't spotting them, or the smaller fish are staying out of trouble in secluded backwaters, smaller pools, or beneath undercut banks. In other words, the sort of places where anglers sight fishing really aren't looking anyway. From a strictly scientific point of view, Stelfox says it can also be the case that often there's just not enough biomass (read: bugs) in the mountain rivers to support large numbers of small trout. In a sense, it's a case of first-come, first-served, and smaller fish dare not show up at the dining table until a spot opens up or more food is served.

Based on my observations in New Zealand (and along the mountain rivers in Oz), I think all of these theories are valid at one time or another. The New Zealand lowland rivers, like the stretch of the Twizel I fished with Fife and Dave, were generally more fertile and had lots of small fish in them. In fact, walking along a stagnant backwater of the Twizel right beside the town one afternoon, we unexpectedly came across a small pool filled with eight- to ten-inch trout. I had similar experiences along other prairie streams and spring creeks. By contrast, along ice-cold mountain rivers like the Worsley and the Travers, I didn't see any small fish at all.

A misconception about Kiwi flyfishing is that the trout are extremely difficult to catch. Sometimes that's true, but not always. I did some really stupid things—lined fish, walked past them along the bank, pulled hooks out of their mouths—and still caught trout that by rights I shouldn't have. When it comes to spooking fish, things actually aren't much different in New Zealand than they are in North America. Isolated trout on remote waters are quite forgiving; trout routinely "bombed up" next to a highway bridge aren't. Angling pressure breeds caution, and it doesn't matter whether you're talking about bonefish on the flats or rainbows in a stocked pond.

BAA BAA BLACK SHEEP

Walking into a strange pub in a strange town in a strange country is not unlike cresting a hill, discovering an unfamiliar trout stream, and wondering where first to cast your line.

A dozen strange faces looked me up and down as the heavy door swung shut behind me. Stepping from the bright sunlight into the dim interior was temporarily blinding, but gradually the faces became distinguishable. They didn't look happy. Leaning my backpack against the wall, I walked over to the bar and straddled a stool. The bartender looked at me like I'd just robbed a bank.

"A pint of dark ale, please."

He moved slowly, deliberately, and asked where I was from. I told him.

"Canada," he mumbled. "I reckon that's all right then."

The endorsement was enough to set the regulars at ease; the talking resumed. Although it crossed my mind, I didn't have the nerve to ask the bartender what would have happened if I *wasn't* from Canada—if I *had* robbed a bank. A rugby match blared from a TV in the corner of the room. It must have been a nothing game, though, because few patrons were paying attention. I engaged in small talk with the bartender and a couple of locals to either side of me. The draft beer tasted good, leaving a white foam ring around the inside of the mug as I drained the glass. The bartender gave me directions to the caravan park north of town, and I retrieved my pack and stepped back out into the midday sun. The door slammed shut behind me; the town was deathly quiet. I was glad the sun was out because the autumn breeze felt cool. I set out across the street in the direction of the Oreti River.

Mossburn and its suspicious pub patrons are located on the South Island, just south of Otago. While the town sees its fair share of anglers over the course of a season, the larger crowds inevitably wind up either farther west at Te Anau, where I'd just come from, or southeast at Gore, which straddles the famous Mataura River and boastfully calls itself the "Fishing Capital of the World." A bit presumptuous, perhaps, especially when the Oreti has brown trout every bit as big and flows through some of the most picturesque terrain in the country.

I don't know if Norman Rockwell ever visited New Zealand, but if he had, the Mossburn area would have provided a virtual gold mine of character and relief. This is vintage New Zealand. Sheep by the thousands. Game farms with red deer and wapiti behind tall wire fences. Mountains wavering on a blurred horizon. Wind-swept prairie grass. Rolling foothills. People as tough as the land they farm.

And, of course, rabbits. Central Otago has its own bucolic charm, but I'll always remember it as the site of the Great Easter Bunny Shoot. You see, the year I was there, a dozen Otago farms turned loose teams of hunters to shoot as many rabbits as possible over a twenty-four-hour period. The Easter Bunny lost a lot of relatives that weekend—8,900 to be exact. In all, more than seven tons of wild rabbits, possums, and goats were bagged by the winning team from the Haast Gun Club. For its efforts, the team received $1,000 with a $500 bonus for shooting the most possums.

The wind was blowing and the power lines whistling as I left town and walked along the shoulder of the two-lane, paved highway. Before long the road crossed the Oreti, and I stopped to gaze over the railing, staring at the braided pools and riffles below to take measure and prepare to pit my ability against what the river had to offer. It looked interesting. On the other side of the bridge I startled several dozen sheep and they scattered, bleating and running fifty yards or so before turning to scrutinize me with their perpetual, idiotic smiles. Fecal smears coated their behinds. Some people think they're cute; I don't. A red ute sped by, slowed, stopped. A burly man dressed in a tattered plaid shirt and wool trousers jumped out and asked where I was headed. I told him. He said he was going that way and offered a lift. Four possums lay in various contortions on the bed of his ute, their heads smashed but two still kicking out spasmodically and swirling their thick, bushy tails in the air.

"Watch out for the bloody spots," he said, genuinely concerned about the state of my pack. "I think there's a clear spot in the corner back there." I pushed a writhing possum out of the way, tossed my pack in the ute, and hopped in.

"I trapped 'em last night," the man explained. "They're making a bloody mess out of my trees." In addition to the money he made from possum pelts, the man also raised chickens for eggs and bees for honey. Quite a versatile character, I thought.

He dropped me off at the caravan park, and I bid him farewell. The front office was empty, but a small sign said to select a campsite or trailer and the manager would be by later to collect the fee. I spotted several tiny one-room cabins, each no larger than a bedroom, and chose the one farthest from the office and driveway. It had two single beds, a bunkbed, a table, and a chair. In a corner there was a portable electric heater with a worn cloth cord and two glowing elements. The floor was made of wooden planks and was partially covered by a small orange throw rug.

I unstuffed my sleeping bag and threw it on a bed, careful not to let the bottom hang near the heater. Bored, I headed back outside. The park was surrounded by a windbreak of towering spruce trees, but the stiff nor'wester ripped through the boughs, scattering fluffy white seed-balls and reminding me of those sheep running across the field. It was far too windy to fish; instead, I set out across the lawn to chat with the only other person in sight, a German named Svend. He'd been taking advantage of the sunny weather to clean a powder blue sedan that he boasted he'd bought for $525 and hoped to sell in two months for $470. On the front dash lay a German edition of Jack Kerouac's *On the Road.* He saw me looking at it and smiled.

"This is me," he said. "On the road." He shook out the last floor mat and asked if I'd like to drive into town with him for groceries. I'd just come from there, of course, but figured what the heck and climbed in. There was nothing better to do. We drove past the saddlery and petrol station to the local dairy, or convenience store. An entire wall was taken up by videos, and a quarter of those were pornographic. Even the heart of rural New Zealand had its scars to bear.

The next morning broke calm and clear. I set out in the direction of the river across a field covered in clover. Starting at the same bridge I'd crossed the day before, I walked slowly upstream along the southern bank, scouting the water for fish through the waist-high grass. Since the bank abutted the highway, access wasn't a problem. The braided river was several hundred feet wide, but it was late in the season, the water was low, and the channel nearest me looked more like a large stream than a river.

The first brown trout I spotted hung a few feet off the bank in two feet of water. It was dark and conspicuous, and since I'd seen it from at least fifteen feet downstream, I took my time setting up for the cast. That was a mistake, however, because no sooner did I begin feeding line out in the current below me than the trout bolted. When the same thing happened with another fish several minutes later, I realized that this wasn't going to be as easy as I'd thought.

Those Oreti fish below Mossburn either had eyes in the backs of their heads or fed backwards, because I never did come close to catching one. Perhaps they were just "bombed up," being right next to the road, because even those I had a chance to cast to ignored my offerings, either spooking straightaway or luring me into a false sense of optimism before closing the door in my face. Humiliated and desperate, I even tried swinging a Woolly Bugger downstream to a sighted fish, but lost the trout and the fly in the sun's glare and could have hit the trout on the head for all I knew.

Eventually, enough was enough. Tensely placing the four sections of my rod back into its cloth sack, I took a sandwich from my day pack, scrambled up the bank to the highway, and set off for the same pub which had welcomed me with closed arms. I was in the sort of mood that, if there had been a bank nearby, I might have robbed it.

Back at the caravan that evening I had another chat with my pal the possum trapper. It turned out he'd worked out a deal with the owners to keep the park's do-it-yourself kitchen stocked with fresh eggs and honey. It was an honor system of sorts, people able to help themselves and put their money into a small tray on top of the fridge. Amazingly, it worked. The trapper said people rarely stole anything, which probably says more than anything else about the nature of Kiwis as opposed to North Americans.

And Lex and Lynn Lawrence, the park's proprietors, were as good-natured as they come. I finally had a chance to meet them that evening when they showed up at the park with two sheep dogs, New Zealand's answer to the cutting horse. The dogs leaped out of the truck before it came to a standstill and bolted across the lawn after a couple of mottled brown-and-white chickens. The frantic chickens knew something the sheep didn't, however; they ducked under a trailer and peeped out at the dogs as the barking hounds ran circles around the covered wagon. This was one instance where the settlers weren't budging.

The Lawrences introduced themselves and I immediately took a liking to them. He was short with reddish hair, calloused hands, and an endearing swagger that would have looked equally at place on the eighteenth green (with his yellow golf sweater on) or knee-deep in sheep manure. She was dark-haired, lively, and tended the park like a well-kept garden. They were the sort of couple that, while palatable enough as individuals, gained something in combination, like white wine and fish.

When I told Lex that I was in the area to flyfish he led me into the office and pointed to a bulletin board smothered in snapshots of smiling anglers cradling big fish. A stuffed silvery brown trout hung on the wall behind the cash register, weighing over ten pounds before styrofoam had replaced blood and guts. Regardless of that morning's futility, it looked like I'd come to the right place. And Lex, it turned out, was the right man.

"I flyfish myself," he said. When I told him about my frustrating day on the Oreti, he explained that I had indeed handicapped myself by tackling the stretch below town, which by that late in the season, had been flogged thoroughly enough to educate the trout in all manners of deception. Lex said the next morning after tending to chores— the Lawrences also operate one of the largest sheep stations in the area—he'd drop by the park and drive me to a spot downstream where I'd probably have better luck.

That's exactly what happened. Lex drove me across one or two miles of private farmland before I began fishing, and the results were immediate. I'd barely had a line on the water before a small brown rose to take a size 12 Irresistible. Two other trout I netted that morning were over twenty inches, thick and silver. One of them watched the same dry fly drift over its head at least five times before rising to take it, sending a plume of water streaking across the pool as the reel protested the line's departure. In fact, I probably would have gone on catching fish all day if a bank of cumulus clouds hadn't intervened, ruining the sight fishing.

That night at the park I had a long talk with Ron, a Montana Bighorn River guide who'd been to New Zealand five years earlier and never really shaken the hook. He'd returned for the season, bought a car, and was talking about buying a house to use as a base. New Zealand can do that to a person. He introduced me to another angler from Oregon, and the three of us spread maps across a kitchen table and exchanged the names of rivers with the same guardedness as pirates divvying up the spoils. Ron had fished several times with Lex, and said if I got the chance not to pass it up.

I got the chance the next day. Lex invited me to fish with him for a couple of days near the junction of the upper Mararoa and Windon Burn rivers. I'd been eyeing the region on a map for weeks but still hadn't figured out how I was going to get there short of hijacking a tour bus or— Lord forbid!—renting a truck. Lex's offer solved the problem. He picked me up in a yellow Nissan 4x4 (if it wasn't an antique, it was close), and we followed the Oreti upstream toward the Thomson Mountains and Mavora Lakes Park. The road deteriorated the farther we went; by the time we reached North Mavora Lake, it was little more than a rutted four-wheel-drive track. The valley there is treeless, the land folded like a dishrag dropped on the counter. Wild grasses lie down to let the wind pass by; negotiating the spongy ground is like walking on sourdough bread. I'm sure some would call it stark and inhospitable. I marveled at the naked beauty.

We settled into Carey's Hut near the end of the lake, unloading our gear, then climbed back into the Nissan and followed the precipitous track down a series of switchbacks to the Mararoa valley bottom. Between the "V" where the two rivers joined, on a prominent ridge, a large stand of trees immediately caught my eye. They were the only trees for miles around, and I asked Lex about it.

"It's called Shirker's Bush," he said. "During the First World War, a family hid there to avoid conscription. That's how it got the name." Recalling that WWI had lasted several years, I wondered aloud if the poor family had at least managed to sneak down to the river to catch a fish or two.

"I don't know about that," Lex said. "But these hills were crawling with game back then, so I reckon they had plenty of tucker." Because the introduced deer had lots to eat and nothing to fear except man and overpopulation, he said they thrived on the grassy hillsides until the helicopters came along. Then, betrayed by the same exposed terrain that had sustained them for so many decades, the deer cullers shot them by the thousands in an attempt to balance nature's scales. These days, Lex said, most of the shooting is done during a regulated hunting season.

We parked the truck and started fishing a couple of hundred yards below the huge pool where the Windon Burn tumbles into the Mararoa. The sky was clouded over and, walking up either side of the sixty-foot-wide river, we stared intently into the inscrutable pools and runs to try and spot fish in the dull light. It was tough but not impossible, something Lex proved by taking a three-pound brown on a small nymph. When we reached the confluence we decided to fish up the Windon Burn and leave the Mararoa until the next morning. I hadn't walked more than ten yards along the small, boisterous stream when a trout darted out from the gravel shore. Actually, I'd seen it but had dismissed it for a dark rock just under the surface. We hadn't walked another twenty yards when Lex did the same thing on his side, practically kicking the trout out from under his foot.

"Geez," I yelled across to Lex. "Every damn fish in this river is lying on the bank." Knowing where to look, a few minutes later I spotted another brown trout lying perfectly motionless along the water's edge. It looked dead, and I was mortified to think that the only fish I might have a shot at that afternoon was beginning to rot. Because it was upright (a posture dead fish rarely assume), I figured it might still have the presence of mind to take a fly.

The trout was lying with its snout behind one awkwardly situated rock and its tail just in front of another; drifting a fly over its head was impossible. Besides, its eyes couldn't have been more than an inch beneath the surface, and I didn't want to drag the tippet over its head. Compromising, I tied on a small nymph and cast out into the current so the fly would sweep by the fish's side. Lex, meanwhile, had crossed over and crouched behind a shrub on the bank to orchestrate the proceedings.

The beige wool indicator was just bobbing along between the two rocks indicating the trout's lie when Lex yelled, "He's taking it!" And indeed he was. The surprised brown raced across the river, head-bucking and digging its jaw into the stream bed to try to throw the hook. Applying steady pressure, I reached into a chest pocket on my vest and handed Lex the camera.

"Try and get a vertical shot if you can," I told him, taking a quick look up the river valley and deciding that was the way to go. That's exactly the picture he got. And it *was* a great shot except for one thing: the fish wasn't in it. The fish, almost forgotten amidst all my fumbling and directing, rubbed the hook from its jaw and swam away unseen.

"That'll be a great picture, mate," Lex reassured me. "You have a really pissed-off look on your face."

That night, back at the hut, we'd just finished doing the dishes when Lex grabbed his rod and wandered down to the lake shore. He said the browns often cruised along the drop-off at dusk. I went too, but spent more time watching him and taking in the sounds and smells of nightfall than fishing. Once in awhile, I'll take off for a day's fishing and not really do much fishing at all. You tell people you're going fishing because—well, because you've got a fishing rod under your arm and a Stetson on your head.

But there's more to fishing than fishing—a phrase only an angler can begin to understand and a phrase only an angler would want to. Sometimes, not very often, I get a feeling while fishing that everything good in the world has condensed and settled upon my consciousness. Everything that matters is there, focused, teetering on the brink of comprehension. In a strange way I suppose it's like the feeling someone gets just before dying.

The next morning Lex fried up bacon off a wild boar he'd shot a couple of months earlier. It was lean and satisfying. He raved about my small white-gas stove, amazed at the amount of heat it put out and how quickly it boiled water. (A couple of months later, just before leaving New Zealand, I mailed it to him as thanks for the trip.) We made the bumpy ride back to the rivers and started fishing the Mararoa just upstream of its junction with the Windon Burn. The morning was still, the grass weighted with dew as the sun slowly climbed into the sky.

I heard it several minutes before I saw it—a vehicle, engine straining as its driver geared up and down in the direction we'd just come from. When it came into sight on the shoulder of the mountain, two things roused my suspicion: First, the Land Rover was red with a white roof, and second, the driver was a maniac. Bob Vaile! Who else could it be? Sure enough, the truck lurched down the side of the hill, jolted to a stop, and out jumped Bob, garbed in his familiar khaki shirt and shorts.

"What the *hell* do you think you're doin' on my fuckin' river, BOY?" Lex started laughing and gave me a look like, 'Who the *hell* is that?'

I introduced him to Bob and Bob introduced us both to Bruce, another Canadian who'd come over to fish with him for a couple of weeks. Out of all the rivers and lakes on the South Island, they'd picked the Mararoa.

"Where are you headed?" I asked.

"Oh, about a hundred yards up around that bend," Bob joked. He stared at the river over my shoulder. "Maybe you guys should back up and cast to that fish you just walked past." Lex and I wheeled around. The large shadow of a nice brown trout had drifted out into the middle of the river to feed. I looked at Lex and he looked at me.

"We just spooked that one," I hastened. "He must have moved up." Vaile, who wasn't buying any of it, just snickered.

As soon as the Land Rover disappeared around the bend, Lex and I scrambled back to the river. A second fish and a big eel appeared in the same emerald pool, which was deep and about fifty yards long. Neither fish was lying still; both cruised slowly upstream, one near the surface and the other barely visible along the bottom. Because Lex had a dry fly on we decided he should have first crack at the pool. Doubled over on the bank, he snuck up behind the fish near the surface and flicked a Royal Wulff onto the water. The undercut bank dropped off steeply beneath him and Lex couldn't see what was going on without leaning over the edge, so I watched from the far bank and told him where to aim his casts. The fish seemed to be ignoring the fly, but, for no apparent reason, suddenly tilted on its axis and angled upwards to take a closer look.

"He's coming up," I hissed. "Don't move, don't move . . ." The trout hung beneath the fly like a marionette, suspended by doubt, then seized fate in its jaw. "*Now!*"

Lex struck. The water frothed. The other fish, the one on the bottom, darted wildly back and forth like a pinball before disappearing under the bank. The eel did nothing. Maybe by that late in the season it had seen the show before. I crossed the river at the tail of the pool and came over to net Lex's fish. A thick hen, it measured twenty-two inches. We took pictures, and this time there was a fish to augment the scenery.

That was it for the day. One fish. We saw half a dozen others, skulking in deep pools or fleeing across rust- and jade-colored weed beds, but hooked nothing. On the way back to Mossburn and the caravan park, Lex kidded me about the score, 2-0.

"Yeah," I said, adding yet another entry to my mental list of New Zealand skunkings. "Sometimes I feel like the black sheep of Kiwi trout fishing."

Joe Wilson had to cancel at the last minute. Owner of the Puha Palace, an historic backpackers' hostel in Mangaweka on the North Island, we were supposed to go fishing together on the Rangitikei River. But business called, and when Joe left for the river that morning, it wasn't to fish but to throw people off a perfectly good trestle bridge with an oversized elastic band tied around their ankles. It's called bungee jumping, and if New Zealand isn't the ritual's birthplace (there's no justification for calling this a sport), it's certainly its adopted home.

People jump off bridges everywhere here. It's big business. It all started when Kiwi A. J. Hackett jumped off the Eiffel Tower in 1986, drawing worldwide attention. Since then, Hackett has made a multi-million-dollar business out of assisting people in jumping off bridges, both in New Zealand and abroad. If you're thinking of committing suicide in grand fashion in New Zealand, don't jump off a bridge: no one will notice.

After my trip, back home, the friends and co-workers who asked me about bungee jumping outnumbered those who asked about flyfishing five to one. "I didn't do a bungee jump," I'd tell them, and they'd give me the sort of look you'd give someone who traveled to Paris and didn't see the Eiffel Tower. Truth is, although the thrill of plunging over two hundred feet into a narrow gorge appealed to me, I quickly realized that bungee jumping is a colossal rip-off. A basic jump goes for upwards of $50. Then they'll try to sell you a T-shirt, still photograph, and home video—all for more money, of course. I decided the money I saved from not bungee jumping would go a long way toward financing a fishing trip. That's what I told people, anyway.

However, don't fret, because there are lots of other ways to perish in New Zealand, many catering especially to tourists. Kiwi entrepreneurs will do anything for a buck; tourists will do anything to oblige. Tandem sky diving, jet boating, parasailing, hang gliding, whitewater rafting, blackwater rafting (in a cave), horse trekking, heli-skiing, heli-tours, sailing, kayaking, scuba diving, swimming, swimming with dolphins, whale watching, rappelling, rappelling upside-down from buildings, mountain biking, windsurfing, hydrospeed-boarding, mountaineering, ski touring—all are for hire at some place or other.

If you ask me, New Zealand is overrun with tour operators, guides, and outfitters. A do-it-yourself trip there is walking three blocks from the bank to the travel agency. Worse, many of the aforementioned activities are having a detrimental impact on the fish and the fishing. Some rivers, like the South Island's Shotover near Queenstown, are so overrun with rafts, jet boats, and helicopters that they've practically been abandoned as viable fisheries. The fish in the Wilkin River south of Makarora are being threatened by jet-boat operators ferrying people back and forth from upstream huts. The wake continually smashing against the banks is causing erosion that's damaging spawning beds. And the list goes on.

New Zealand is a strikingly beautiful country with much to offer, but the tourism racket is getting out of hand. The government must find a compromise between participation and conservation. Kiwis also should keep a simple tenet in mind: if there's nothing left to look at, no one will come.

NORTH ISLAND BLUES

The first clue came as I was waiting at the Taupo airport with a fishing rod. I was booked to fly into the central North Island's upper Ngaruroro River, and because fishing was foremost on my mind, I had a fly rod. Nothing strange about that, except that mine was the only fishing rod in sight. The rest of the fellows sitting around the waiting room at Taupo Air Charters had guns. There were bolt-action rifles lying across laps. There were semi-automatic rifles leaning against the wall. There was even a rifle of undetermined action being fondled by the filthy hands of a demented-looking teenager. I felt badly for the rifle: I felt even worse for his girlfriend.

The hunters were dressed in red-and-black plaid or drab green or khaki or any of the other colors generally associated with firearms and shooting things. They sat sprawled in chairs or stood against the walls with blank, slightly pained expressions. The whole scene—the guns, the men, the boy—reminded me of one of those Third World guerrilla units waiting for something to happen; which, based on the number of photographs depicting guerrilla fighters lying around in the jungle smoking cigarettes with idle looks on their faces, apparently doesn't happen very often. The hunters were lying around, one impatiently explained, because high winds had grounded the helicopter that was supposed to transport them to their chosen fields of battle. Of course, that should have been the second clue, but I didn't pick up on it at the time. Even with a bright blue windbreaker and sissy fishing rod, the hunters welcomed me into their ranks. I guess I should have been grateful.

Looking back on it now, there were all these clues hitting me over the head, yet I still climbed into the front seat of that single-engine plane with the demented-looking teen and his proud father in the back. Their rifles, I noticed, were packed away in the tail; I was happy for that.

"Do your seat belts up *really* tight," the pilot told us. Another clue. She obviously knew something that we didn't. We taxied down the runway, nosed into the wind, and the plane shot skyward faster than a kite in a stiff breeze. "Make sure that seat belt's *really* tight," the pilot repeated, and I knew then we were in deep trouble.

The situation deteriorated about ten minutes into the half-hour flight. We were skirting the beech-forested Kaweka Mountains, headed south, when the plane began bucking like a mechanical bull. I yanked my seat belt down so tightly I carved a notch in my shoulder, and still my hair brushed the roof every time we hit an air pocket. The creaking plane had jolted the teen's cockiness into moribund silence, but suddenly the worst of it was over and the pilot banked heavily and the trees disappeared and there, a silver rivulet in a golden, grass-covered valley, lay the Ngaruroro.

The teen and his father were headed to a hunting camp farther up the valley and were off before I'd unloaded my pack from the plane. The pilot humored me and snapped a picture of me standing beside a wing strut—the brave angler! Then she jumped in, taxied back up the grass strip, and disappeared down the valley. The wind quickly stifled the plane's drone; the only sounds were a nearby orange windsock snapping in the breeze and the rustle of bobbing prairie grass. Looking up at the south wall of the valley, I spotted the backcountry hut beneath the jagged spires of the Boyd Rocks. The wall as far up as the hut was devoid of large trees but covered in manuka and other hardwood scrub. Behind the hut, between it and the climb to the rock spires, was a large stand of beech trees. There was a steep rip-rap staircase leading to the hut from the airstrip, and that's where I headed.

Boyd Lodge is to New Zealand huts what the Taj Mahal is to tombstones. It sleeps sixteen people in two rooms separated by a spacious, well-appointed kitchen. As fate would have it, however, I spent three nights there alone. A large wooden deck and railing wraps around the front of the lodge, and the view of the Ngaruroro River valley makes climbing all those rip-rap steps worthwhile. The only drawback seemed to be these neat little turd piles evenly spaced along the top of the railing and outside the bunkroom doors. Picking up a broom and without giving it much thought, I swept the offensive pellets off the deck. So much for that, I convinced myself, completely unaware that I'd just committed the first act of war.

Because I had some time to kill before supper, I decided to go fishing. I really wasn't sure how I was going to cast in the strong wind, but I figured I'd worry about that later. What angler can resist the tug of new water, especially when it's laid out before his eyes and reputedly holds rainbow trout the size of small salmon? I set off downstream because that way I could fish my way back up to the airstrip and avoid a long trudge at day's end. But what had looked like easy going from the plane turned out to be a slog. The feathery pampas grass didn't pose any problems; the boggy ground beneath it did. The landscape was pockmarked by slippery water-eroded ravines, well-disguised marshy lowland, and strange white cliffs towering above turquoise pools. Terrain my eyes told me could be covered in fifty paces took one hundred; what looked like level ground from a distance was scarred by depressions.

After less than two miles of this I turned around, said "Screw it!" and began to fish. At least, I went through the *pretense* of beginning to fish but actually didn't do much fishing at all. That's to say, I walked along the bank with my fishing rod angled carefully backwards, scrutinized every pool through my brown Polaroids, and spotted . . . absolutely nothing. The river was empty. The trip was a sham. "How can I get my money back?" I asked myself, suspecting that the folks back at the Taupo airport were having a good laugh at my expense.

There was a time that first afternoon, just once, when I thought I'd sighted a fish. It was lying there with its nose on a white rock, and I snuck up behind it with the stealth and determination of a sniper who knows he's only got one round in the chamber. I crouched on the bank and tried several nymphs without success. I tried dry flies, stood up, even tried waving my arms in the air above my head. The fish still lay with its nose on the white rock. I was moved; the fish wasn't. So, naturally, I reached down, plucked a stone from the bank, and tried to bean it. There was a feeble splash and the stone, which, come to think of it, *had* seemed rather light for a rock, floated away like a sailboat. I rubbed my eyes, laughed, and examined another bleached-white stone. Pumice. I'd been had. The fish wasn't a fish and the rocks were rafts.

After amusing what was left of my sanity for a while with the floating rocks, I continued walking the river and eyeballing empty pools until, in a moment of sheer frustration, I said "Screw it!" again, cut up a ravine, and worked my way back to the hut. Obviously, I thought, the next day held two choices: fish upstream or fish way, way downstream. Then I recalled that the demented-looking teen and his dad had gone upstream to hunt. The choice was easy.

No sooner did the horizon extinguish the sun each evening than the temperature began plummeting. March is a fall month in New Zealand (the equivalent of September in North America) and the lodge's wooden beams cracked and settled as the cool night air sucked the afternoon heat from the swollen timbers. The flies disappeared in a swipe, the wind dropped, and the valley was still and quiet. I stood on the deck and watched as darkness lay its gentle hand upon the landscape and shielded it from view. When there was nothing left to look at, I wandered into the hut and lit a fire in the pot-bellied stove. That's where I cooked my supper, tearing open a fifty-pound sack of coal and piling the greasy chunks into the stove until the black edges caught fire and glowed with a devilish intensity.

I was lying in my sleeping bag that first night, long after the timbers had stopped contracting, when a sharp *thud* jolted me awake. Something had dropped from the roof onto the deck. It clattered along the boards and came to a standstill outside my door. I half expected the crazed teen to come barging in with his smiling father in tow, but no, this creature was much too cunning for barging. It was a possum, I knew, and even though it wasn't about to turn the knob and walk in, I nonetheless wondered what the heck it was up to out there. I was just about to jump up and find out when the clattering resumed and the varmint wandered off. Satisfied, I fell asleep.

The next morning there were three shiny turd pellets outside the bunkroom door. There were more pellets along the deck railing and outside the kitchen door, and the possum had left small streaks of urine scattered along the deck. The little bugger, I told myself. This means war—and I'm not about to lose to a possum with a grudge!

But enough of that already. The morning was fine. Fish awaited. I packed lunch and some spare clothes, struggled into my wet Buller boots, and headed off downstream. The plan was to stay on high ground along the sloping valley for as long as possible before dropping down to the river to begin fishing. However, it soon became obvious that the high ground wasn't necessarily dry ground, and before long I was forced down to the river to wade, slog, and curse my way along the overgrown banks. Below the confluence of the Ngaruroro and Gold Creek, the valley constricts and the riffled currents of the upper river are funneled into a steep, shrub-choked gorge with translucent pools and long shadows.

Creeping to the edge of a thirty-foot cliff, I poked my head over the side and stared into a beautiful blue pool. I saw it immediately. The large gray shape slowly worked its way toward the head of the pool; then the trout turned, drifted downstream to a point just ahead of a shallow gravel fan and circled back upstream once again. The trout tilted slightly to steady itself, and for a split second the dark riverbed was sundered with a red gash that instantly healed itself and left a luminescent scar on my mind. It was a rainbow, all right— a bloody big rainbow at that.

I watched the trout complete another lap in its watery express-way, then slithered down a narrow, steep ravine to the pool's tail. From that angle I could only see the fish when it dropped down and started swimming upstream again, so I figured I'd wait until just after it circled, lob a nymph about ten feet ahead of the trout, and keep my eyes fixed on the wool indicator. That's exactly what I did, but the fish ignored the nymph on the first pass and I changed flies while waiting for it to complete another circuit. Sure enough, it reappeared with the stealth of a submarine, and I shrank into the green ferns and grass as it turned broadside. Its eye was large and probing. Somehow it didn't see me.

I made two quick false casts, trying to keep the line against the rock wall and well away from the middle of the pool, then angled the leader so the fly plopped dangerously into the water on a collision course with the fish. The nymph sank and the trout struck hard. The line shot through the guides and the fish made a strong run to the head of the pool. Then it stopped. It came downstream just as quickly, unsightly coils of green line gathering at my feet as I scrambled to take up the slack. The fish rushed to the tail of the pool and cleared the water in a sickening, spectacular leap. It hung suspended in the air for a moment, like David Carradine in *Kung Fu*, then toppled backwards. I picked up line, but there was nothing on the other end. The fly was free.

There were other pools that day, other sightings. But I didn't land a fish. They were spooky, to be sure, but I had my chances. If it wasn't one thing it was the other. The cliffs were too steep. The water too deep. There were too many footprints in the sand, no doubt left there by the last party of heli-anglers. By late afternoon I'd given up. It was dusk by the time I got back to the lodge. I swept the turd pellets off the deck and splashed water on the urine. Somehow the possum's antics didn't seem as funny as they did that morning. The little bugger was going to pay.

The possum took the offensive. I was losing at solitaire, as usual, when it clattered up the steps. I blew out the candle and inched toward the glass kitchen door with a broom in one hand and my headlamp in the other. The possum shuffled to a stop and, throwing the door open, I framed it in the beam of light. It cowered a bit and stared at me like a black Garfield. Since I've never been fond of the cartoon cat anyway, there was little remorse when I brandished the broom like a sword and rushed at my foe. But it scurried away and, to be honest, I held back at the last moment. I couldn't bring myself to deliver the fatal blow. Throw floating rocks at would-be fish, yes; kill a cheeky possum, no. I'd given it a good fright. No doubt it wouldn't bother me again.

The next morning the deck was covered in poop and piss. Outside the doors, along the railing . . . everywhere. I cleaned it up, ate a cold breakfast, and headed downstream, begrudgingly impressed, boldly determined. I tramped even farther than the day before—tramped for two-and-a-half hours until the gorge forced me down to the river and my destiny. It was cool in the shade and I jumped up and down and shook my arms to try and jump-start my circulation.

I spotted a nice rainbow right away, but it was against the far bank and I couldn't wade out far enough to make a decent cast. Just upstream, I came to a very deep pool with two or three fish feeding along its length. The one at the rear was holding near the surface, so I gambled and tied on a size 14 Irresistible. The leader turned over nicely and the fish dropped back several feet beneath the fly before sipping it in. I waited until its nose disappeared and dug the hook into its mouth. The rainbow shot forward as if it had been propelled by a cannon, skimming the surface and sending the other fish fleeing for cover. Then it got off. The worst-case scenario had taken place before my disbelieving eyes. That's pretty much how things went the rest of the day. A repeat of the day before. There was only one certainty as I walked back to the lodge that evening: the possum was going to pay. Again.

It struck just after nightfall. No fooling around this time. I discovered that, for some reason, I could shine my headlamp right at the possum through the front windows without disturbing it. I watched it advance, waited until the critter was poised to poop outside the kitchen door, then sprang my ambush. I swatted the possum in the ass as it ran along the deck and jumped onto the top railing. I was just about to deliver the death blow when it gave me a look that stopped me cold. There was hatred in its eyes, and I was truly frightened. I mean, I was carrying a *broom*, for Christ's sake! I could see the headlines: ANGLER MAULED BY CHEEKY POSSUM: TURDS FOUND ON BODY!

It stared at me a moment longer, then leaped onto the roof and vanished. Shaken, I retreated. The possum must have known it had me rattled, because it launched an offensive the likes of which hasn't been seen since the Gulf War. It paraded up and down the deck at will, wise to my tactics now, pooping, pissing, spitting, and hissing. It was all I could do to make it to the bunkroom. I was under siege. The next morning I withdrew, heading in a northeasterly direction to the Oamaru River valley and safer ground.

It's about a four-hour tramp from the Ngaruroro River to Oamaru Hut. Amazingly, the moment I crested the side of the Ngaruroro valley, the tussock plains vanished and the path descended into a towering mountain-beech forest. The sensation was no different than, say, opening the door of a greenhouse and walking into a blast of Arctic air. During a water break beside a small stream, while relaxing in a grove of tree ferns, I met the first people I'd seen in almost four days: a group of three hunters, two carrying rifles and the other a longbow. If not for the rifles the three men could have passed for Robin Hood, Little John, and a really ugly Maid Marian. The merry trio was headed in the opposite direction, to Boyd Lodge, and asked if anyone else was using the hut.

"No," I replied, "just the possum. It's got the hut all to itself now." I told them about the three-day feud. They laughed, motioning to their guns, and said they'd take care of the cheeky possum. Even my wily adversary, I knew, couldn't withstand such firepower. I surprised myself by feeling badly but realized the futility of asking the hunters to spare the possum. If it was any consolation, there were plenty of other territorial pissing possums just waiting to claim the lodge as their own. Life goes on.

Oamaru Hut isn't as lavish as Boyd Lodge, but it has a hominess about it that's hard to resist. From the front porch, an angler can see the Oamaru River to the south, the Kaipo River to the north, and the upper Mohaka River, which begins where the other two join, to the east. The rivers meet at the hut and so do the people. In the fall you're liable to share a bunkroom with anyone from a hunter to a sheepherder. As for myself, I shared the hut with Arthur, a man fully capable, I convinced myself, of burying a hatchet in someone's skull.

The funny thing is, Arthur looked like a fifty-year-old page boy. His black hair, flecked with silver, turned in on itself like the lip of a waterfall. Patchwork stubble sprouted from his chin, and his beady eyes, set deeply in a chiseled face, darted furtively around the room like a rat's. But it was Arthur's right hand that intrigued me most. There, tattooed across his knuckles, was the word L-O-V-E. One letter to a finger. Dark green and dangerous. Occasionally, as Arthur rambled on in a Kiwi vernacular so incomprehensible that I didn't have a clue what he was saying, I'd stare at that right hand and wonder how many people had been L-O-V-E-struck courtesy of a well-placed uppercut.

Arthur loved to talk. Angling his legs and wool sock-clad feet in front of the pot-bellied stove, he'd sit and shovel coal and bull shit in equal proportions until either one or the other ran out and it was time to go to bed. Poaching was a favorite topic; like the time Arthur spotlighted a red deer then threatened to beat the crap out of the landowner when he drove up to complain. Oh, he had stories all right! Barroom brawls. Naughty sheilas. Welfare checks. For some reason, Arthur took a liking to me. I was his buddy. A little crazy for fishing during hunting season maybe, but hey!—what the hell. We all have our problems.

My immediate problem, of course, was trying to catch a fish. The weather had turned lousy, and snow muzzled the peaks when I woke up the next morning. I probably should have stayed in front of the stove with Arthur, but I only had a few days left until the plane would be back to pick me up, so I bid him adieu for the day and wandered down to the Oamaru. The water was up and slightly off-color. Still, finding I could cross back and forth at will, I worked up whichever side put me over the best water and cast to several small brown trout. Despite the murky water, they were skittish and spooked easily. I didn't hook any. When my hands got too cold to change flies, I called it quits.

Arthur was sweeping the hut out when I returned. In addition to being a lunatic, he was meticulous. I made some hot soup, rediscovered my circulation, and decided to try the Kaipo. It's nothing more than a stream, really, emerging from the forest amidst a tangle of deadfall where it meets the Oamaru several hundred yards downstream of the hut. The manuka trees along the banks were impenetrable, so I found the going easiest in the water. It was absolutely calm and I spotted the first fish on the inside corner of a long, grassy bend. The tiny waves originating at my feet ruffled the water over the fish. I thought it was game over. But when the surface calmed the trout was still there. Casting a nymph into the pool would have had the subtlety of lobbing a hand grenade into a department store, so I opted for a dry fly. My six-weight rod and weight-forward line proved too much, however. The leader struck the water sharply, and the fish bolted for cover in an underwater snag. What a mess. Not far upstream I spotted another fish lying on the gravel just inside of a sharp eddy line. Cautiously approaching it from almost directly behind, I stopped over thirty feet away and started to remove the fly from the hookkeeper. Taking my eyes off the fish momentarily to grasp the hook between my fingers, I looked back up and the fish was gone. What had I done? What *hadn't* I done?

That night Arthur admitted that he'd abandoned a group of buddies camped in tents farther up the Kaipo. Apparently they'd had a falling-out of sorts; he didn't elaborate and I didn't ask. The group was hunting by day and drinking by night, and the next morning a helicopter was scheduled to fly three sheilas into the hut to round out their little party. Arthur was bitter, no question.

"Bloody bunch of jokers," he snapped. "I 'ope they get the clap, each and every one of the bastards!"

I really didn't want to be around when the Merry Pranksters showed up to collect their booty, so I cleared out bright and early on another remarkably dull morning. Fog rolled down the Mohaka River valley as random snowflakes dropped from the sky like shooting stars. My fingertips teetered on the verge of frostbite, red and damp. They say that wool fingerless gloves are just the ticket on a day like that, but I think you're better off either stuffing your hands into your pockets between casts or wrapping them around a steaming cup of coffee. It's been my experience that all fingerless wool gloves do is get soaking wet and let you watch the progress firsthand as your fingers turn red, then purple, and finally chalk white.

The day had a monochromatic feel and look to it which was quite disturbing. Seeing into the water was difficult. The Mohaka riverbed, which is much too swift and deep to cross in most places, is sculpted from volcanic rock. It's beautiful to look at but treacherous to wade. The brown trout like to lie along the seams of these beige-, pewter-, and gold-colored depressions, making them almost impossible to spot. I'm sure the local guides have it all figured out, but between the weather and the river itself, I only managed to cast to three or four fish all day. One of those pulled a stunt that basically made me pack it in for the week. A nice brown, it held just inside a large eddy where the river surged against a black rock wall. The reflection of the wall from the far bank muted the silvery glare on the surface of the water, so it was actually quite easy to spot the fish working in the shallow water. I was able to approach from well back along a gravel bar without spooking the trout.

I tied on a size 12 Pheasant Tail nymph and made a nice cast. Not too far so that the fly caught in the main current and swept into the rock wall; not too short so that the fly landed on top of the fish. A nice, decent cast. The indicator skimmed across the water, and I saw the fish swerve at the fly beneath it. My arm tensed, anticipating a strike. But the next thing I saw was the fish bolting clear across the river to the shelter of a submerged rock shelf. There was only one explanation: the fish had eyeballed the fly, seen the hook, and figured things out. I was rattled again, and there wasn't a possum in sight. Or so I thought. As I walked back across the meadow to the hut, the sound of a barking dog was immediately followed by the crack of a rifle. There was a whine in the air above my head, and I dove to the ground and hunkered behind a small rise. Arthur, I thought. He's finally lost it, and he's shooting at me. But how to explain the dog? There was another shot and then there was silence. I lay on the ground for several minutes, scared silly, then peered through a small tussock to try and see what was going on at the hut.

There was the group of them—Arthur and the Merry Pranksters— and they were laughing and waving something black and furry in the air. The dog was still barking frantically. I arrived at the hut about fifteen minutes later.

"You missed all the fun," Arthur said excitedly. "The sheilas came and my mates came to meet 'em and we treed a possum and shot it out of the branches."

"Where is everyone?" I calmly asked, deciding not to mention that they'd almost shot an angler out in the meadow as well. Arthur said the group had just left for their campsite up the Kaipo. He wasn't going, he explained, because sheilas or no, he had no intention of freezing his butt off in a tent when a pot-bellied stove and fifty-pound sack of coal were so close at hand.

So be it. The danger had passed. Arthur hadn't lost it. Only one more night, and I'd be safely on my way out of that valley forever. I'd gone almost a week and spent over $175 in airfare—without catching a fish. But hey! I still had my life, didn't I? Surely that must count for something.

I honestly think that Arthur was sad to see me go. He moped around the hut, sweeping dirt into a pan and telling stories, as I stuffed things into my backpack and broke down my rod. Then I set out across the Oamaru River, soaked my feet for the last time, wrung my socks on the far bank, and climbed the steep hill to the airstrip. The odd cloud sent rain spattering down, but other than that the sky was blue. I might have been imagining things, but I thought most of the rain clouds were passing right over my head. The plane was almost two hours late.

Looking back on it now, there were all those clues hitting me over the head, yet I had still climbed into the front seat of that single-engine plane with the demented-looking teen. At least I hadn't seen *him* again. The flight out was without incident. All in all, I'd have to say it was the smoothest part of the trip.

If you took all the people on the South Island, rounded them up, and plunked them into an empty city, its population would only slightly rival that of Auckland's 840,000 inhabitants. With a landmass one-quarter again larger than the North Island, the South Island is home to less than a third of New Zealand's 3.35 million residents. What I'm getting at here is that if you value wide-open spaces and uncluttered water, the South Island is the place to go.

Most of the foreign flyfishers I met were of the same mind, including those who'd done several trips to both islands. To be frank, I think a lot of the North Island's appeal has more to do with nostalgia than anything else. The Tongariro River, which flows into Lake Taupo near the geographic center of the island, is a storied trout stream, perhaps the most famous in the country. There's no denying that it's still a good fishery, with large annual runs of rainbows up from the lake. But I was disappointed with the couple of days I spent there. Well-worn trails line both banks, and almost every good pool and riffle was crowded with anglers. Besides, I'm always skeptical of a river crossed and paralleled by a state highway, where every pool shown on the map has a name. When the pools are named things like Lonely and Never Fail, I get downright suspicious.

Nevertheless, Lake Taupo and Lake Rotorua, its neighbor about an hour's drive to the north, are probably the most popular stillwater fisheries in the country. Anglers have been known to can and bottle fish on site at Lake Taupo, which still produces over twelve hundred tons of trout annually. If posh lodges and salmon-style chuck-n-duck flyfishing are what you're after, either lake is definitely worth a look. Conversely, if, like me, you're after more of a do-it-yourself backcountry experience, the North Island options are limited.

Because the fall "roar," or rut, was in full swing and the woods "chock-ablock" with deer hunters, common sense prevailed, and I curtailed my fishing several weeks before I'd planned, in early April. One of the casualties was an anticipated week-long tramp into Urewera National Park and the upper Waiau River and its tributaries. I had a park ranger to thank for backing out: he told me that if I went into the heavily forested area dressed in drab green and crept along streambeds, then I might as well go all the way and strap a pair of antlers to my head. Point taken.

FAR FROM THE MADDENING CROWD

I was keeping the mice awake. I knew that because there it was, well after midnight, and they were running back and forth over the end of my sleeping bag. Others scurried across the tin roof—*rat-tat-tat-tat-tat-tat-tat*—and still more scratched at the wallboard behind my head. It was mice pandemonium, and I, laid out on the floor like a sacrificial victim, was smack-dab in the middle.

The alpine hut, tight on the bank of the upper Buller River, was called Teetotal, a total misnomer if ever there was one, because the only things more numerous than the mice were the empty beer cans scattered around the floor. The hut had seen better days. The walls were coming apart at the seams. The prefabricated metal fireplace, riveted to the rest of the hut like an afterthought, had come unhitched. The roof leaked. Things stank.

Making matters worse, the fishing had been lousy. It had been raining a lot lately; the olive-colored river was high and murky. I'd spent several hours poking around the likely looking spots earlier that afternoon and hadn't seen a fish. Before long I was casting blind—a last resort in New Zealand. The upper Buller, located just north of Nelson Lakes National Park and west of St. Arnaud and the Yellow House, is a daunting piece of water. Wading is treacherous on the cow-pie-slick riverbed; the banks are smothered by brambly wild blackberry shrubs and matagouri. Unless the fishing is really on or you really know what you're doing, it's probably a good idea to hire a guide. If nothing else, he'll steer you away from the Teetotal Hut. That piece of advice alone is worth $100.

Fortunately, for every Teetotal there are ten—no, make that fifty—top-notch huts spread around New Zealand. In fact, the huts are so extensive you could walk clear across both islands and never have to spend the night outside one. I'm convinced that as far as backcountry accommodation is concerned, New Zealand's huts are the best deal in the world. When I was there, a season's pass cost about $35. Some of New Zealand's most exclusive fishing lodges (places where $35 wouldn't get you past the bellhop) are merely a short walk from some of the nicest huts. For a complete run-down on the huts, the best place to go is any Department of Conservation office. (Kiwis sometimes refer to this as the Department of Constipation, but I won't get into that.) Both Auckland and Christchurch have DOC offices with all the information you'll need.

The great thing for the angler, of course, is that just about every alpine river of note in New Zealand—and there are dozens—flows within tramping distance of a hut. The Greenstone, Wilkin, and Travers rivers come to mind on the South Island; the Mohaka, Ngaruroro, and Waiau rivers on the North. There are many, many more. The end result is that you don't have to mortgage the wife and kids to afford accommodation on a New Zealand fishing trip. What the heck, bring them along. Children's annual hut passes are half price. Just be careful where junior sticks his nose. Fishing with Bob once near the headwaters of a remote South Island river, we started rummaging through a stack of mildewy magazines in a hut and came across a *Playboy* from the mid-sixties, no doubt left there by a very lonely sheepherder. There wasn't a pubic hair to be seen (that wouldn't come along until 1969), and many of the photos were missing as well.

Unfortunately, Tassies and the mainland Aussies haven't kept pace with the Kiwis when it comes to backcountry huts. There aren't many, and what huts there are along the good Australian trout streams are generally dilapidated and best used as emergency shelters to wait out storms. You can't really blame the Australian parks and wildlife service for this, because money is tight and distances are vast. (The mountain ranges along the mainland's southeast coast, which sustain the only viable trout stocks, comprise a mere fraction of the total landmass.) Besides, Australia never undertook the massive deer cullings that gave rise to New Zealand's fabulous hut system. Sometimes, good things *do* come from bad.

In Oz, tenting is the operative word. Selecting a tent is as personal as buying underwear, so I'll try to avoid the methodology of tent selection. I will, however, offer a few tips. First, get a sewn-in floor. As you're undoubtedly aware by now, Australia is crawling with beasties. A fellow I met at a flyfishing shop told me he'd been sleeping soundly in his floorless tent one night when he awoke and rolled over. Something moved under his elbow. He froze. It froze. He didn't say how long they stayed that way, the two of them, but I got the impression he didn't fall back to sleep. Neither did the snake. Eventually, it slithered out and the man's heartbeat returned to normal.

Spiders can be a problem, too. Especially the tarantula-sized funnel web, whose bite is just as serious as and should be treated just like a poisonous snake's. It's mouse-sized hole looks pretty inconspicuous until you inadvertently go to pitch a tent over it; then it looms large. I did that once with Will Spry in the Snowies.

"Whoa!" he yelled, just as I was shaking the tent out to get it square on the ground. The cloth snapped as I yanked it back up. Sure enough, there it was—a spider hole. A pair of beady eyes stared out at us from the shadowy lair.

"We'll have to find another spot," Will calmly said, unsure whether the spider was in fact a funnel web but not wanting to take any chances.

Yet another tent tip is to never, ever believe anyone who tells you a tent is one hundred per cent waterproof. It's a lie. The worse kind of lie, because given the right set of circumstances, it could incite you to commit violent acts against the salesperson. The only waterproof tent is a rubber tent, and no one wants to sleep in a condom. Use this general rule of thumb: if a tent can "breathe" (a word salespeople love), it can "leak" (a word salespeople hate). Seams can only take so much slashing rain. Condensation is a direct by-product of perspiration and breathing (yours, not the tent's), so even if a tent doesn't "leak," that doesn't mean you won't have water running down the inside of the walls. A well-ventilated tent with a fly is the best compromise between weight and water-resistancy (note I didn't say waterproofness). I'd avoid the single-wall designs at all costs: I've had nothing but trouble with them.

So much for the backcountry. Just as important is to know where to stay *between* fishing stops, in the cities and towns. In a word: hostels. It's as simple as that. Both New Zealand and Oz go out of their way to cater to low-budget travelers. To the penny-pinching angler sallying about with a fly rod on his back, this is a God-send. In addition to the international Youth Hostelling Association, both countries also have several private hostel chains, often referred to as "backpackers" accommodation. These are ubiquitous and always worth a look. In Canberra, I stayed in a hostel so lavish it felt like I'd tripped and fallen into the Hyatt. It had a large sun deck with umbrellas, a huge lounge, and mountain bike trails out the back door, all for about $10 a night. In Hobart, I stayed in a hostel fashioned from a nineteenth-century house. The hosts, two ne'er-do-wells who dressed like the Blues Brothers and watched the movie every second night, were fashioned circa 1980.

Yet another option in either country are the numerous caravans, which I've already mentioned on several occasions. These are often on the outskirts of town and cater primarily to people with vehicles, but many also rent cabins and parked trailers. In addition, most have spots set aside where you can pitch a tent for a couple of bucks and use the kitchen and showers. Special weekly rates are often available, so if you're going to be fishing in the same area for awhile, it might be worth checking to see if there are any caravans about.

Of course, the ultimate prize for any shoestring traveler is still a freebie: the old, "Oh, why don't you come and stay at my place for the night?" Don't laugh, it happens. Not often, but you can increase your chances by being sociable and by hanging out a lot at fishing shops and pubs. You'll be amazed how friendly the locals get after a pint or two. Act destitute. Play poorly at darts. People take pity on a charity case.

Or, if you'd prefer, just wander around until you bump into someone you know. A couple of days before I flew out of Tasmania, I popped into a Hobart sporting goods store to pick up a few supplies. There, squeezing the insulation on a polyester sleeping bag in a city of 180,000 shoppers, stood Colin. Needless to say, he was as surprised to see me as I was to see him. He asked me to stay the night at his place, of course, and suggested a last-minute fishing trip to the Tyenna River, located about an hour's drive west of Hobart near Mount Field National Park. So the next morning, on cue, we hopped into the old white Benz and rigged up together for the final time. The sky was cobalt blue; any animosity between us had been left behind in the Central Highlands. There was still a hint of competitiveness, but of the good-natured, healthy variety that intensifies an outing rather than subverting it. We fished as friends and equals. And the fish obliged—scrappy foot-long brown trout that rose for any well-presented dry fly that we cared to tie on.

The Tyenna is small and forested, but the water was exceptionally clear and you could see the trout through the leafy green branches we parted to scout the pools. Unable to cast from shore, we leapfrogged our way up the river, taking turns at especially nice pools we happened upon at the same time. Later, in the afternoon, Colin watched from shore, laughing, as I missed three consecutive strikes on three trout rising in the cool shadow of an overhead bridge.

"You're pulling it out of their mouths," he said. "Count to three and then set the hook." Given the circumstances, there was nothing to do but agree. It's tough to plead innocent when you're holding the smoking gun.

I've got a picture in a slide catalog somewhere of the kindest couple in Oz. It just so happens that they're standing in front of the largest rainbow trout in Oz (a lifelike, twenty-foot-high sculpture in the town square at Adaminaby), but that's not the point. The point is they deserved much more than that $50 glass rod I gave Tom and Jean as a way of saying thanks.

The fishing had been spotty all week along the Providence Arm of Lake Eucumbene. The anglers out trolling in their eighteen-foot cruisers were returning each evening with a few decent fish, but we shorebound types weren't faring as well. The only success I'd had was by playing hide-and-seek with the trout along the flooded shoreline deadfall come sunset. I hooked a few; landing them proved more difficult. It would have been easier trying to thread a needle with a haystack. What I really wanted was to get the heck out of there, either east to the Murrumbidgee River or, better yet, all the way to Canberra and that new graphite rod I'd ordered by phone. Only one problem: there was no public bus service, and no one seemed to be heading in my direction. Certainly not Tom and Jean. He came over to my tent one chilly morning, threw back the flap, and invited me for a hot breakfast.

"How's bacon and eggs?" he said.

"Sounds great to me."

They were staying in a trailer they kept year-round on the beach at Angler's Reach. As the name implies, it's a small village and popular fishing destination—basically an assemblage of weathered cottages, shacks, and trailers spread along the Eucumbene lake shore. Handing me a steaming mug of coffee, Tom and Jean settled back into a worn couch, and we swapped tales while the wind sent tremors up and down the trailer's metal walls. I talked and talked and talked. It was bloody cold outside, and I didn't want to leave my newfound nest.

"So where are ya off to next, mate?" Tom asked.

I told him. He looked at Jean and they excused themselves, slipping into the kitchen and asking me if I wanted another coffee. A minute later they re-emerged, asking me if I'd like to drive with them into Cooma, a town of about eight thousand people farther east that would put me some seventy miles from Canberra. Jean said it was too cold to fish that morning, and they'd just as soon go into town to gamble a few dollars away. I knew that they'd never intended on leaving the trailer, but what could I say? Out on the lonely two-lane highway, they made a point of stopping at every landmark, including a brief look at Australia's only llama farm. When they dropped me off at the caravan park Jean took me in her arms and hugged me, her bushy white hair piling against my cheek. My mother's name is Jeanne, and they reminded me of each other, so the hug seemed a bit like a surrogate.

"You take care, now," she said affectionately. I knew that I'd never see either of them again.

Everyone's heard the horror stories about hitchhiking. The proverbial *bad ride*. I'm sure things like that happen, and if I was an attractive woman, I'd just as soon show up solo at a rodeo as stick my thumb out on the side of a road. Nevertheless, in my opinion, this "fear of thumbing" is highly overrated. As with almost everything else in life, let common sense be your guide. Don't take a ride on a motorbike without a helmet. Don't take a ride from a driver without pants. Good, common sense.

Hitching, after all, is a really cheap way of getting around. Sometimes it's the *only* way. This is especially true in Oz, where the last stop on the scheduled public bus service is often the first stop for the serious angler. Hitching is also a great way to meet people and remind yourself what a small world we live in with some five or six billion inhabitants.

"Sure, I know your cousin," the owner of that Snowy Mountain rafting operation—the guy who might have saved my life during the wasp episode—told me during our van ride through the Snowies. "He lives in Canmore, right?"

"Uh huh."

"I met him in the Philippines. It must have been the same guy. I'm sure it was him. What's his name . . . Jim? Jack?"

"Jeff."

"Jeff. Yeah, I'm sure it was him."

Hitching a lift on a semitrailer is great because the view is panoramic. And truckers, I'm convinced, are the most interesting people in the world. Something about all that open space liberates their minds. They also have lots of time to think things over, and that helps, too.

The hitching in New Zealand is strictly second-rate. For starters, the country is a lot smaller with just as many if not more budget travelers, so the competition can be fierce. There's a real art to learning how to jockey for position on the roads leading out of town; fistfights have been known to occur. Bring a good book, a soft pack, and be prepared to wait for hours. One fellow I met outside the Yellow House claimed that he'd been trying unsuccessfully for two days to hitch a ride out of town. The last I saw of him he'd changed his travel plans and was headed in the opposite direction, toward the pub.

A better alternative in Kiwi country is to take the bus or, wallet permitting, rent a car, van, or RV. The New Zealand highways are extensive. And owing to the number of young travelers, the two or three national bus lines in New Zealand ensure you'll never have to wait more than a day no matter where you're headed. If you do decide to go the rental route, thoroughly research the access to the river or lake you plan to fish. A lot of New Zealand's best water lies at the end of some pretty dubious terrain; a 4x4 definitely helps.

Even when the four-wheel-drive paths give out, however, someone in New Zealand always seems to find a way to take you one step farther. Many of the large lakes have water taxis, anything from a souped-up ski boat to an ocean-worthy cruiser. A few rivers, like the South Island's Wilkin, offer transportation via jet boat. And then, for the really wealthy or the incredibly desperate, there are the airplanes and helicopters. Despite the risk of being labeled a hypocrite (I did a fly-in trip on the North Island), I have mixed feelings about both. We've all heard countless stories about the fabulous Kiwi fly-in fishing. No doubt most of them are true. But lots of Kiwis and a few tourists to boot are starting to seriously question whether they want New Zealand's alpine headwaters sounding like the opening scene in *Apocalypse Now*. After spending that stint at the Oamaru Hut with Arthur and his gang, I realized what a menace helicopters could be.

Some Kiwis, such as angling author John Kent (his two guidebooks to the North and South Islands are the best I came across by far), are urging the government to set aside special wilderness zones where helicopters are prohibited. I'm all in favor of this. Too often, a fit angler spends a day or two tramping into a remote river only to watch a helicopter land just upstream and jettison its unfit cargo. Money can buy a lot of things in life, including large fish, but it shouldn't be able to buy *everything*! Both the United States and Canada restrict the use of helicopters in national parks, and New Zealand should do likewise. The outfitters would loudly protest, of course, but they make up a small percentage of Kiwi outdoorsmen catering to a limited clientele. Let them tramp.

Besides, access is only part of the story. What about aesthetics? Who wants to spend a tranquil day astream listening to the *thump-thump* of rotor blades passing overhead every second hour? And what about the animals? Does anybody care about the stress they endure?

Yet, despite the pestilent planes and helicopters, anglers still enjoy an amazing amount of freedom in New Zealand. On the South Island, at least, private waters are few and far between. And the landowners, whose stations often rival the famed Montana ranches in size and beauty, will rarely turn an angler away if you ask permission and show respect. In over four months spent fishing there, I can't recall being turned down. To someone used to seeing his share of No Trespassing signs in North America, the amount of unposted land in New Zealand is remarkable. Without question, the biggest threat to New Zealand angling is the as-yet-unspoken notion—shared by a few half-witted Kiwi guides—that foreigners be banned from fishing there without a guide. This is absurd, mainly because, as Kent points out, the average overseas flyrodder is more conscientious when it comes to catch-and-release than his Kiwi counterpart. I'm sure plenty of foreign anglers would still make the trip, and there's no doubt a guided angler catches more fish in New Zealand (or anywhere else, for that matter) than an unguided one. However, personally speaking, I'd still like the option of figuring a few things out on my own instead of spending the entire trip staring down a pointed finger. Besides, I wonder how the freedom-loving Kiwis would react if we did the same to them.

By and large, the Australian attitude is more relaxed, at least as far as the guides are concerned. The landowners can be a bit unruly, likely out of suspicion more than anything else. Most of them just don't see that many flyrodders. A few pockets of resistance still exist among the farmers flanking the Snowy Mountains, but after chatting the landowner up for a minute or two, he or she will usually relent. In Tasmania, of course, the biggest problem may be *finding* the landowner. A lot of the countryside is pretty isolated. And while you'll need consent to fish some of the best water in the farmland districts—creeks like Brumbys near the town of Cressy—most of the best stillwater fishing is hassle-free. That's especially the case in the Central Highlands, and even more so in the Nineteen Lagoons district.

Thankfully, all of the streams, lakes, and lagoons in the more remote Western Lakes area are now protected under the new Central Plateau Conservation Area, revised and expanded in June, 1990. The result is that the entire area now falls within either a national park or World Heritage site: access is restricted to a few bouncy four-wheel-drive tracks and wherever your lungs and feet can take you. No helicopters interrupting your afternoon siesta here, just ravenous flies, venomous snakes, ants an inch long, and weather that makes the Rocky Mountains feel like Miami Beach.

Even paradise has an entrance fee.

OTHER FISHING TITLES
FROM JOHNSON BOOKS

PIKE ON THE FLY
The Flyfishing Guide to Northerns, Tigers, and Muskies
Barry Reynolds and John Berryman

FLIES FOR ALASKA
A Guide to Buying and Tying
Anthony J. Route

FLYFISHING ALASKA
Anthony J. Route

POUL JORGENSEN'S BOOK OF FLY TYING
A Guide to Flies for All Game Fish
Poul Jorgensen

ANGLER'S GUIDE TO AQUATIC INSECTS
AND THEIR IMITATIONS
Rich Hafele and Scott Roederer